This is an important book that will encourage Christians to enter into a deeply personal relationship with our Lord Jesus Christ. This is a superb book.

- Lyle Dorsett
Best-Selling Author and Pastor
Retired Billy Graham Professor of Evangelism at
Beeson Divinity School, Samford University

Where were these insights twenty years ago? Jamie Moore reveals in one masterfully written book what it took me more than two decades to figure out on my own. The ripple effect from these truths will change many lives.

- Jeff Lyle
Author, Teacher and Pastor
Transforming Truth Ministries

FRIENDSHIP

with

GOD

FRIENDSHIP
with
GOD

*Discover God's Relational Presence and
Receive Peace, Identity, and Purpose for Your Life*

JAMIE MOORE

DOXAZO

Free Resources for Readers
The *Friendship with God*
Discussion Guide and Video Course
(Over 2 hours of video content from Jamie)

The chapter-by-chapter discussion guide and video course are both designed to help you practically apply the principles of this book in your daily life.

These resources are absolutely free to you!

The discussion guide is available to be purchased in paperback online, but you can receive a free digital copy at:

https://www.jamiemoore.org/friendshipfreebies

The video course is available for individual or group use. You can get free access to the video course at:

https://www.jamiemoore.org/friendshipfreebies

To Abba

You roared over me.

I will roar for you—forever!

CONTENTS

THE FRIENDSHIP WITH GOD FRAMEWORK

Have you ever wondered why you feel alone, even when surrounded by a crowd of people?

Have you ever counted your "friends" on social media but have a gnawing sense that none of them knows you? Not the real you, anyway.

Have you ever been physically present with someone—but not relationally present? And after several minutes of conversation, you realize you haven't heard a word they have said?

Have you ever felt like a chameleon—changing your identity based on what other people think about you? To some, you are brave and bold, and to others, you are sweet and kind. But you're not sure which you actually are.

Have you ever been paralyzed by fear and felt there was no one you could talk to or rely on to help? Or have you ever gone all day with a looming shadow of anxiety you cannot explain or identify?

Have you ever experienced ravenous boredom, searching for something to entertain you but unable to find anything that satisfies?

Have you ever felt such shame and regret that you hide and pretend you no longer exist? Or force a smile on your face and pretend like nothing happened?

I have. All those. And lots more too.

I have also felt frustrated by my lack of intimacy with God.

I have wondered why everyone else was "feeling" Him but I was missing out somehow.

I have heard others talk about "hearing" God's voice, and I would smile and nod, pretending to be gifted in this way too.

I have read the Bible and learned about individuals called "friends of God" who had partnered with Him to do amazing things—all the while I myself felt an underlying dissatisfaction in my relationship with God. I was bored, disconnected, ashamed, and afraid.

This book is for those who have ever felt like that. Bored with God. Disconnected from others. Ashamed and hiding the real "you" from everyone, even your Creator.

FRIENDSHIP WITH GOD

Everything changed when I discovered that God created me to be His friend. He created me so He could be with me. He *wants* to be with me. And He wants to be with you.

God desires to be intimately involved in all aspects of your life. He desires to experience your day with you. His desire is to be your friend. He likes you. He wants to commune with you. He wants to be with you every day of your life.

I know that sounds impossible. How can you be friends with a divine being, especially One you cannot see? How can you be friends with a holy and righteous God when you are so messed up on the inside?

For a time, I was puzzled by this. I cried out and asked God to help me understand how to be closer with Him. Honestly, at times it seemed He wasn't listening. Or I wasn't getting it. Either way, we weren't friends.

Over time, though, I discovered a framework for friendship with God that He showed me in His Word. That's what this book is about.

FRIENDSHIP FRAMEWORK

In short, friendship with God grows exactly like every other friendship. It takes three things: time, conversation, and activity—together. Every friendship requires these three ingredients. The best of friends have spent hours in each other's presence. They talk with each other. And they "do stuff" together.

Time + Conversation + Activity = Friendship

If even one of these ingredients is missing, the friendship struggles. For example, if my friend and I never spend time together, we feel disconnected. If we spend time together but never talk or do anything, our friendship is stagnant and boring. If we talk but are never together and never share a common goal, our relationship suffers.

Think about a championship winning team. After the game, the star player is interviewed and says, "I am so proud of my guys. We've worked for this all year. We talked about what this moment would feel like and how to get here. We did it! I could never have done this without my guys. We're family. And I'm so happy to share this with my team." Did you see the ingredients? The team became a family of friends because they (1) spent hours together in practice, (2) worked on their communication, and (3) had a mission to accomplish together. The same is true for your friendship with God. Growing in friendship with Him means spending time together, talking with each other, and working together every day.

This book is an invitation to start a friendship between you and God. In section 1, you will learn how we got to this place of disconnection from God and others and what He has done to pursue friendship with you. In section 2, you will learn how to practice God's presence every day and spend time with Him. In section 3, you will learn how to hear God's voice and talk to Him. In section 4, you will learn the purpose God has planned for you and how you get to partner with Him in this adventure.

Deep friendship with God is not only possible, it's why He created you. I am evidence of a cultivated friendship with Him, and daily I grow more peaceful, more secure in my identity, and more excited about what God and I get to do together.

The Father told me to write this book. We wrote it together. I am confident that if you will read and put into practice what is found in these pages, your life will be changed forever. You will be awestruck at the goodness of God. You will experience freedom from paralyzing fear. You will discover your true identity and live secure in God's love. You will hear God speak to you every day. You will walk in peace. You will be present with those around you. You will see the supernatural power of God flow through you to others.

You will become a friend of God.

Part One

WHERE ARE YOU?

So when [Eve] saw that the tree was good for food, and that it was a delight to the eyes, and that the tree was to be desired to make one wise, she took of its fruit and ate, and she also gave some to [Adam] who was with her, and he ate. Then the eyes of both were opened, and they knew that they were naked. And they sewed fig leaves together and made themselves loincloths.

– Genesis 3:6–7

Chapter One

PRESENCE LOST

And they heard the sound of the LORD God walking
in the garden in the cool of the day, and the man and
his wife hid themselves from the presence of the LORD God
among the trees of the garden.

– Genesis 3:8

You were created to enjoy God and be His friend.

That statement may sound crazy, but it's true. We see this in the Bible from the very first book. God created everything and called it *good*. He created people and put us in a garden. Why? Was it to have workers, robot-like servants, to do His gardening? Was He bored and thought, "Let's create something and have some fun—who knows how it will turn out?"

No, He created you so He could be with you as a friend.

We see this in the garden of Eden. God created a place of beauty and put Adam and Eve in that place to be with Him. They walked together. They talked together. They laughed and played together. They enjoyed each other's company. They cultivated the garden together. They named the animals together. They dreamed of how they could make the garden even more beautiful— together.

Adam and Eve enjoyed the presence of God, walking with Him in the cool of the day, hand in hand, seeing each other face-to-face. They were friends.

Everything was perfect and good. Not only were the garden and the animals good but togetherness was good. Vulnerability was good. Looking at God face-to-face was good. Working with God in the garden was good. There was no hiding. No shame. No miscommunication. No insecurity. No anxiety. No loneliness.

The first man and woman experienced friendship with God and friendship with each other. It was perfect and good.

WHERE ARE YOU?

Then something happened. The Bible tells us that one day God was doing what He always did—walking in the cool of the day—but Adam and Eve were not there. Where were His friends? They were no longer in His presence. They were no longer with Him. So, He went looking for them.

Adam and Eve heard God walking in the garden, and they were afraid. They were now fearful of the One they had walked and laughed and talked with, and were hiding in the bushes. God called out, "Friends, where are you? Adam? Hey, Eve? I am here to walk with you like we always do. Where are you?"

This is a heartbreaking moment, isn't it? You can hear the pain in His voice: "Friends, where are you?"

Of course, God knew exactly where they were—physically and emotionally. He knew they were afraid and ashamed and hiding from His presence. He asked the question "Where are you?" because Adam and Eve didn't quite understand where they were. God hadn't changed— they had. God was coming to walk and talk with His friends like He always did. But now they were hiding from Him.

HOW DID WE GET HERE?

In Genesis 3 we hear the story of a serpent who hated God and His friends. He wanted to destroy the relationship they had. So this serpentine liar set out to cut off the lines of communication. He whispered to Eve, "Can you really trust this 'friend' of yours? He's keeping things from you. He doesn't want you to be happy. Look at this tree and the beautiful fruit on it. Doesn't that look so good? You should take it and eat it."

What was the enemy of God and His friends doing? He was lying to Eve and trying to convince her that her "friend" wasn't very good at all. The serpent was accusing God of keeping good things away from Eve. He was persuading her to think of God not as a friend but as a rule-maker who could not and should not be trusted. The serpent wanted to destroy the relationship between God and His friends.

SHAME COVERINGS AND HIDING FROM GOD

So Eve took the fruit and ate it. Then she gave some to Adam, and he ate it too. God had said this would bring death, and it did—but not right away, of course.

First, it brought shame. Adam and Eve now realized they were naked, and they became ashamed of showing their true selves in front of each other. Sinning against God brought them shame.

Second, they attempted to solve their shame problem by sewing fig leaves together as coverings for their bodies. Before eating the fruit, Adam and Eve were naked and unashamed. Afterward, they felt shame and tried to cover up. These fig leaves kept them from being fully seen and fully present.

The shame coverings weren't enough, though. They heard God walking through the garden, and they became afraid. They didn't want Him to see them. They were afraid of being seen. They were ashamed, so they hid from God. The consequence of their sin was the inability to be fully present, either with God or each other. Sadly, they lost friendship with Him.

THE ENEMY'S SCHEME FOR YOU

Let's take a break from that story for a moment. I want to be a friend and a help to you right now. The tactic the serpent used with Adam and Eve is the same one he uses with you and me today. He hasn't changed. He wants to steal, kill, and destroy you and all your friendships (John 10:10).

A secret of success in war is to know the strategy of the enemy. This is why decoding secret communications between enemy forces has been a big deal. Likewise, if you could discover the enemy's plan of attack and location, you could change your strategy and move your troops.

The enemy's scheme is to cut you off from being fully present with God, your family, and your friends. He wants you ashamed, anxious, and hiding your true self from God and others.

First, the enemy will twist God's words to encourage you to distrust Him. The enemy will convince you that God is unapproachable, silent, and distant. He does not want you to have anything to do with God. He will distort your family's and friends' words too. He will convince you they don't care. He will encourage you to protect yourself by not being open and vulnerable with them. "If they don't know the real you, then it won't hurt so much when they let you down," he'll whisper in your ear.

Second, the enemy will exploit your feelings of shame and nakedness by suggesting you distract yourself with shiny toys. "Here's a tasty-looking fruit—this will satisfy you!" His suggestion is that if you are too busy working or playing, then you won't feel ashamed, naked, or vulnerable. If you buy a bunch of new toys, you will forget the corrosive shame on the inside.

Third, when the numbing newness of these toys wears off, you will realize that the shame is still present. So, the enemy will suggest that you attempt to cover those feelings with a false self. He will convince you that if you succeed at work or achieve respect, then the feelings of shame will go away. Or he will convince you to pretend and act like everything is fine. If those around you think you are doing well, they won't know you feel broken and hollow on the inside. He wants you looking to fashion fig leaves to cover your shame.

Finally, the enemy wants to keep you on this hamster wheel of leaf-making madness. Keep the masks up so no one knows how broken you are on the inside. Keep lying to everyone so they think you are awesome. It is an exhausting and never-ending battle to keep the fig leaves from falling off and exposing our true selves to everyone— including God.

All this does is leave you feeling alone. No one knows you, because you are hiding. Hiding may feel safe, but then you think, *No one really loves me because no one knows me. If they knew the real me, there's no way they could love me.*

Alone.

WHERE ARE YOU RIGHT NOW?

So, we come to this question: *Where are you?* Are you fully present with God and others—right now? Where are you spiritually? Are you enjoying God's presence, hearing His voice, and walking with Him through your day today? Or does it seem like He is distant?

Where are you emotionally right now? Do you feel God's love for you? Do you feel loved by family and friends? Do you feel known by God and others?

Where are you mentally right now? Where does your mind go when it's free to wander?

Here's a tip: wherever your mind goes when it's free to wander is where you think your shame can be covered. Your mind is searching for something to cover your feelings of weakness, brokenness, and shame.

That's one of the reasons your thoughts obsessively spin at times. Your mind is frantic and seeking a shame covering. *What can make me feel better? Where can I find something to take away this anxiety?*

Where are you right now?

FASHIONING FIG LEAVES

The enemy's goal is for you to feel lost, disconnected, ashamed, and hiding from God and others. His plan is to convince you to try to fix those feelings on your own. The really devious aspect of his plan is that nothing we try works.

Accumulating piles of cash won't work. Achieving influence and status won't work. Numbing your shame with porn, video games, movies, social media, and everything else won't work. It didn't for me. I found myself in the hamster wheel of pornography and shame and then numbing that shame with games, work, achievements, or more pornography. I found myself exactly where I started but feeling worse.

Shame.

Even religion doesn't work. Obeying the rules won't fix your shame. It's just more fig leaves that keep falling off. Money, influence, and pleasure don't work either.

How Do We Fix This?

So, what does work? How do you cover your shame? How do you live fully present—and unashamed—with those around you? How do you enjoy God's presence without feeling He's judging you? How do we fix this?

You can't fix it. Not by yourself, anyway. Any effort on your part to "fix it" will end in failure. Trust me. If you remember nothing else, remember this: trying to put on your own fig leaves never works. That's the bad news.

Here's the good news though. Right after the heartbreaking encounter with His lost friends, God does something. The Bible says, "God made for Adam and for his wife garments of skin and clothed them" (Genesis 3:21).

Did you see that? God made garments to clothe their shame. God fashioned a more permanent shame covering from an innocent animal. God, the Creator, was the first to kill anything in His creation. An innocent animal was killed, and its skin was used to clothe the shame of Adam and Eve.

Our problem of sin and shame has mortal consequences. Our sin is costly, and God has taken on that cost Himself. He has set a plan in motion to cover your shame and sin. He has worked to fix the problem you and I created for ourselves.

We are hiding. We're filled with shame. We have lost the presence of God. We have lost the capacity to be vulnerable with God and others.

We can't fix it.

But the Bible tells the story of God fixing this problem and getting His friends back. The Bible is one epic story of the way God worked to get us back for Himself.

God wants to be friends with you. He wants to be friends again. This means He wants to walk with you and spend time with you. He wants to talk to you. He wants to be on an adventure with you.

He doesn't just love you—He actually likes you. And He wants to be your friend, today and every day.

In the next chapter we will look at the big storyline of the Bible. In a single chapter, you will see what God has done to be friends with you.

We can't fix it, but He can.

Chapter Two

GOD WITH US

I will make my dwelling among you, and my soul shall not
abhor you. And I will walk among you and will be your
God, and you shall be my people.

– Leviticus 26:11–12

My dwelling place shall be with them, and I will be
their God, and they shall be my people.

– Ezekiel 37:27

Behold, the dwelling place of God is with man. He will
dwell with them, and they will be his people, and God
himself will be with them as their God.

– Revelation 21:3

For the past twenty years, my wife, Jess, and I have enjoyed watching a show about castaway contestants on an island. These men and women seek to outwit, outplay, and outlast their competition. It's one of the most popular shows of all time, and it birthed an entire genre called *reality television*. The show, of course, is *Survivor*.

At the start of each episode, host Jeff Probst says three words: "Previously on *Survivor*." This is a smart move as it can be difficult to remember all the characters, plot lines, and intrigue from the previous week's episode. By taking a few moments to remind the audience of where the show has been and where it's going, the directors help orient the viewer, which makes for a more enjoyable experience.

Jess and I love movies too. One of our favorites is *The Lord of the Rings* trilogy of movies by Peter Jackson. What is shocking, though, is that when the second movie starts there is no help for the viewer. *The Two Towers*, the second movie in the trilogy, assumes you know what's going on and are ready to hit the ground running.

Here's what I mean. If you were to turn on *The Two Towers* with no context about the first movie—including hobbits, dwarves, elves, the ring, or the plot—you would be in trouble. You would be disoriented. *The Two Towers* opens with a majestic view of a snowcapped mountain range. You hear screaming. Then the camera zooms inside the mountain, and you see an elderly man with a large stick on a narrow bridge opposite a fiery demon with a whip. The senior citizen in a gray cloak yells, "You shall not pass," and then slams his stick into the bridge. The demon falls, and all seems well. Unexpectedly, the demon lassos the geriatric gentleman and pulls him off the bridge. They fall together, fighting, through the heart of this mountain.

That's it. That's how it starts. No "previously on *The Lord of the Rings*" like in *Survivor*. No help. Good luck—hope you are ready to go because the story is continuing.

Why am I saying all this? (Other than because Tolkien's novels are my favorite books and I wanted to write about them?) The reason is that sometimes the Bible feels more like *The Two Towers* than *Survivor*. In fact, if you don't orient yourself before approaching the Bible, it will take a while to figure out what's going on.

In my experience, if I open the Bible and start reading, it's not helpful. I've learned to stop and reorient myself with a few questions before jumping into the text: Where are we? What's happening? What part of the story am I looking at? Who are the characters in this part of the narrative?

I don't want you to feel disoriented when you read the Bible. I want you to be excited and have some framework about what is happening and what God is trying to say. So, this chapter is all about the "big story" that the Bible is telling and how to get oriented to it before you read.

Before we begin, here's the big idea of the Bible: *God wants to be with you.* Yes, you. And He has gone to extraordinary lengths to be with you.

So, here we go. The big story of the Bible in seventeen minutes (give or take a few minutes depending on how fast you read).

EXILED FROM THE GARDEN (GENESIS 3)

We already started this story in the last chapter. God created Adam and Eve to be His friends and to enjoy each other's presence. They walked, talked, and cultivated the garden together. The enemy tempted Eve to sin against God, her friend. She did. She ate the fruit of the forbidden tree, and Adam joined in this sin too. The consequences of their sin were guilt, shame, and hiding from God. Their relationship with God, their friend, was broken.

In the garden was another tree, the Tree of Life. God understood that Adam and Eve couldn't stay in the garden with Him because of their sin and broken relationship. They were no longer friends. If God let Adam and Eve stay in the garden, they would live forever—afraid of Him and stuck in brokenness.

You may ask, "How would they live forever? I thought one of the consequences of their sin was death." It was. But remember, there's another tree.

God explains it this way. He has to kick Adam and Eve out of the garden and His presence because if they stay they will eat of the Tree of Life and live forever. Forever, but forever afraid of God. They would live forever, but hiding and broken and disconnected from their former friend.

That's hell, isn't it? To live forever but be afraid of the One you live with—eternal hiding.

So God removes them from the garden, His presence, and the Tree of Life. The rest of the Bible, from Genesis 3 to Revelation 22, is the story of God working to rescue and restore His former friends to the garden. He wants them back in His presence. He wants to walk with them in the cool of the day again. He wants to talk with them again. He wants to cultivate the garden again. So He creates a plan to get His friends back.

The shame coverings of animal skins that God put on Adam and Eve were a sign of something to come. God put to death an animal to cover their sin and shame. An innocent animal was sacrificed for their sin. Remember that point. It will be important later.

One final thing. Outside the garden, God placed cherubim and a flaming sword. A cherub is a heavenly being who guards the presence of God, and *cherubim* refers to a group of these guardians. The cherubim and flaming sword have a purpose: guard the way to the Tree of Life. Adam and Eve lost direct access to God and His presence.

TABERNACLE IN THE WILDERNESS (EXODUS 40)

Many years pass. God chooses one man, Abraham, to bless all the nations of the earth. From Abraham comes God's chosen people, Israel. These people were blessed by God to be a blessing to all the people of the earth. God's people find themselves enslaved in Egypt. He hears their cries for help and sends another man, Moses, to set them free.

In a burning bush (notice the flame), God meets with Moses and commissions him to speak to Pharaoh in Egypt and set the Israelites free. God rescues His people from Egyptian slavery and brings them to a mountain called Sinai. There the glorious presence of God comes down onto the mountain where Moses is standing.

God speaks to Moses and establishes some rules of engagement between Himself and the people. He called this a covenant. The goal of the covenant is in three parts: (1) I will be your God, (2) you will be My people, and (3) I will dwell with you.

Did you catch that? God is working to get back into relational presence with His people. He wants to "dwell" with them. God wants to be with them. The word *dwell* carries the idea of habitation, living together, and being together. Sounds like friendship.

God instructs Moses to build a "dwelling place" for His presence, called the *tabernacle* (beginning in Exodus 25). The tabernacle had multiple rooms, and the innermost room was the *holy of holies*. The manifest glory and presence of God came down and dwelled in this room. To keep everyone out, a thick veil was placed over this compartment. Do you know what God instructed them to embroider on this veil? He told Moses to embroider the image of cherubim into the thick veil that covered the holy of holies.

Interesting, isn't it? God's presence was now in the midst of His people while they wandered. That's good. But there was still a separation and an artistic guardian reminder—the cherubim. Sacrifices were made at the tabernacle daily to remind the people of their sin, shame, and separation from God.

God's glory and presence were now among His people in this portable garden-tabernacle dwelling place, but it was still separated. God has more in mind, including a bigger and permanent garden-temple in Jerusalem.

TEMPLE IN JERUSALEM (2 CHRONICLES 7:1–3)

David, the greatest king of Israel, desired to build a permanent dwelling place for God in Jerusalem, the royal city. Eventually, his son Solomon accomplished the building campaign and constructed a permanent temple for God's presence. King Solomon inaugurated this dwelling place with a great sacrifice. In response, the glory of God filled the temple. His presence was so thick that the priests couldn't stand being in the space.

What you need to know about this temple is that it was a large replica of the tabernacle. There was an inner room called the holy of holies, and a thick veil separated worshipers from the direct presence of God. What image do you think was embroidered on that veil? Yep. Cherubim (2 Chronicles 3:14). The artistic portrait of these heavenly throne guardians still communicated separation and distance between God and His people.

On the Day of Atonement, the high priest could enter the holy of holies to make a special annual sacrifice for the people of God (Leviticus 16). Once a year. That's it. God is dwelling among His people, but only one man gets to be in the direct presence of God and only once a year. God is among, but not directly with, His people.

So, this garden-temple is now permanent and fixed in Jerusalem. If God's people want to be close to Him, they must make a pilgrimage to the royal city. But even in the city, most people could never get in the same room as God. He is not accessible directly.

Unfortunately, Solomon's male heirs struggle to lead well as kings. Civil war erupts during the reign of Solomon's son. God's people divide themselves into the northern half of the kingdom (Israel) and the southern half (Judah).

God sends prophets to warn the kings and the people to obey God and not be tempted to serve other gods. The warnings contain a specific threat: if they continue to disobey, God's presence will leave the temple and the people will be captured and sent into exile.

Sounds like the garden again, doesn't it? Adam and Eve disobeyed God, lost His presence, and were exiled from the garden. The prophets are warning that this will happen again.

Years pass, and the people ignore the prophetic warnings. The presence of God does leave the temple, like He warned (Ezekiel 10:18–19). The Northern Kingdom is captured, and the people are sent into exile. Finally, the Southern Kingdom is captured, the temple is destroyed, and the people of God go into exile in Babylon. The people God had created to be with Him are separated from Him once again.

All hope is not lost, though. Inspired by God, the prophets declare a future promise of returning to their homeland and rebuilding the temple. Eventually, the people do return and rebuild the temple in Jerusalem. Unfortunately, God's presence isn't there anymore. Not only this, but He is also silent. For four hundred years, no one hears a single word from God. His presence is gone, and His voice is silent. What will happen next?

That is how the Old Testament ends. In silence. Waiting in hope.

IMMANUEL: GOD WITH US (JOHN 1 AND 2)

The New Testament begins with the arrival of a baby. This baby was the fulfillment of a prophecy written by Isaiah: "Behold the virgin shall conceive and bear a son, and shall call his name Immanuel" (Isaiah 7:14). The name Immanuel means "God with us." This baby was Jesus, who is both God and man. Jesus is the meeting place of God and humanity.

The apostle John explains that Jesus is the Word of God. He wrote, "In the beginning was the Word [Jesus], and the Word was with God, and the Word was God" (John 1:1). Jesus is God and man. John continues, "The Word became flesh and dwelt among us, and we have seen His glory" (v. 14).

Do you see that connection? This Jesus is God, He became flesh like you and me, and He "dwelt" among us. The word *dwelt* refers back to the tabernacle from the wilderness wanderings with Moses.

This passage also adds that the disciples had "seen His glory" (v. 14). What's John saying here? He's saying that God has come in human flesh to be the meeting place where God's glory is directly available to everyone. Amazing!

God walked with His disciples. They talked together. They laughed together. They ate together. They worked together. God was back with His people! His glory was available and accessible to everyone. What's even crazier is that Jesus, the God-man, looks at His disciples and says, "I have called you friends" (John 15:15). God wants to be friends again with us. And this is possible through Jesus.

But how? Well, remember the tabernacle, the temple, and the sacrifices? Jesus calls Himself the temple and says, "Destroy this temple, and I will raise it again in three days" (John 2:19 NIV). What was He talking about? He was talking about His own body (v. 21). Jesus began to predict His own death and said things like, "Greater love has no one than this, that someone lay down his life for his friends" (John 15:13).

And that's exactly what He did. Jesus was crucified and nailed to a tree for the sin of the world. He was innocent but willingly gave up His life for you and me. On the cross, as He died, Jesus cried out, "It is finished." When he said this, "the curtain of the temple was torn in two, from top to bottom" (Matthew 27:51). When Jesus died, the thick veil with the embroidered image of the cherubim was torn from the top down—by God Himself!

Because of Jesus, everyone can have direct access to the glory and presence of God anytime. This is amazingly good news. The cherubim are no longer needed because access to God is now available to everyone!

GOOD NEWS AND GARDENS

Let me talk about Jesus for a second. He's my favorite. He's my friend. He is the good news, and it all has to do with gardens.

You and I were born with the same purpose as Adam and Eve: to be with God, as our friend and father. That's why you were created. And like Adam and Eve, we have sinned against God and lost our innocence. We are broken. We experience shame. We walk in fear of God, others, and the future. We are disconnected and lost. We are exiled as enemies of God when we should be His friends and family. We lost the garden. We lost friendship with God. We can actually "feel" this loss and brokenness on the inside.

We can try to fix it, but we can't. Only God can fix this.

God came in human flesh. His name is Jesus. He lived the life you and I should have lived. He was present with the Father, present with others, unashamed and pure. But even though Jesus was innocent, He was betrayed by a friend of His, Judas. This traitorous "friend" hatched a plan to betray Jesus in a garden called Gethsemane. God, in flesh, working to rescue His exiled kids, was betrayed in a garden.

Not only was Jesus betrayed in a garden but He was also executed on a tree. He was tortured like a criminal, even though He was innocent. He was beaten and mocked. The Romans crucified Jesus and killed Him. God, in flesh, working to rescue His kids who were exiled from His garden, was nailed to a tree. The whole reason we got into this mess was because of a tree. Forbidden fruit from a tree brought a curse on all humanity. God, in flesh, came to die on a tree for you and me.

Not only that, but after Jesus died, He was buried in a garden tomb. (You cannot make this up—this is God's story!) And after three days, He was raised from the dead.

Jesus died for the sins of the world. The Father accepted His Son's death as a sacrifice for my sin and for your sin. But the Spirit worked in the body of Jesus to resurrect Him and bring Him back to life, victorious over sin and death.

A couple of women who followed Jesus came to the garden tomb to anoint Jesus' body. When they got to the tomb, they saw that the stone that sealed the tomb had been rolled back, and the tomb itself was empty. No Jesus. No body. In fact, the resurrected Jesus later walks up to one of the women, Mary, and asks her why she is weeping. She doesn't recognize Him at first and thinks Jesus is a gardener and that He might know where the body has been placed. Do you see it? Jesus is mistaken for a *gardener*. Again, you cannot make this up.

Mary doesn't recognize Jesus until He says her name. When she realizes it is Jesus, she runs and embraces her Savior and Friend.

How about You?

Have you heard Jesus call your name? He is calling right now. You don't have to live in exile anymore. You don't have to live in fear and shame any longer.

Jesus is calling you. He wants you back as His friend. Will you receive Him today?

Stop and thank Jesus for dying in your place, for your sin. Thank Him for being God, in flesh. Thank Him for coming to rescue you and bring you back to Himself.

Jesus is the innocent One who died in your place to set you free from sin and shame and to bring you back into friendship with God. Turn from your fig leaves and your shame coverings. Put your trust in Jesus today. He died for you, in your place, to pay the penalty for your sin and shame. Turn away from hiding and covering shame, and turn toward God in Jesus.

Ask Jesus to set you free of fig leaves and rotten fruit. Tell Jesus you trust Him and that you will follow Him. Stop right now, and spend some time with Jesus.

Living Temples of the Indwelling God

Back to the story. What does Jesus do after He is resurrected? He hangs out with His disciples. He eats with them. He talks with them. He walks with them. He laughs with them. Jesus is back with His friends.

Unfortunately for them, He doesn't stick around. But the story isn't quite finished. Before Jesus was crucified, He told His friends that it would be better for Him to leave so that another Helper could come. At His ascension to heaven, Jesus commissions His friends to go make disciples of all nations. He says, "I am with you always," and then He leaves (Matthew 28:19–20).

What? I can hear the disciples' puzzled thoughts. *You say You are going to be with us always, and then You leave to go to heaven? What is going on?*

Well, the problem is physical.

Think of it this way. If Jesus is the meeting place of God and all humanity, then it would be difficult for more than a couple hundred people to experience God, right? For example, consider when Jesus fed the five thousand. How many of those people felt they got to experience Jesus' presence and talk to Him personally? Probably not many. It's a limitation of being in physical form. But God had a plan for that.

The plan is this: *God Himself will come and dwell inside His friends.* When we turn away from our shame coverings, put our trust in Jesus, and have our sins forgiven, the Spirit of God comes and dwells inside us. Jesus sends His Spirit to dwell within His believers and friends.

It's amazing! The glory and presence of God, which was in the tabernacle and then in the temple, now resides inside you, by faith in Jesus.

The apostle Paul puts it this way: we have become temples of the living God (1 Corinthians 3:16). Our bodies become the temple of God. Our hearts become the holy of holies where the presence of God dwells. We are mobile temples!

PENTECOST (ACTS 2)

In the book of Joel, God promises to pour out His Spirit on all people (Joel 2:28–29). Then, in Acts 2, we read the fulfillment of this promise at Pentecost. After Jesus' ascension to heaven, the entire group of believers was together, praying. Suddenly a noise like a powerful rushing wind was heard, and they each experienced the Holy Spirit coming to dwell within them. They saw what looked like tongues of fire above each of their heads. They were all filled with God's Spirit, and they began to tell others, in other languages, about the mighty works of God.

This was the start of the New Testament church. God filled His people with His presence so they became little temples where His glory would dwell.

But that's not all. Individual believers join with other believers and, together, are built up into a beautiful dwelling place for God. You see, it's not just about you and the Father, Son, and Spirit. It's about you, the Father, Son, and Spirit . . . and other believers together! The church is a gathering of individual temples, all carrying the presence of God.

Together, we become the temple of God—and this dwelling place is once again portable. When the temple in Jerusalem was built, the presence of God was fixed in the royal city. But now, as in the days of the tabernacle in the wilderness, the presence of God is moveable—this time, in royal people like you and me!

This is why we talk about being on mission with God. We join the mission of God to expand His presence and His kingdom all over the world. Wherever we go, individually and corporately, we carry His presence and His kingdom with us. Portable temples, on the move.

That's Acts 2 to present day. This is the part of the biblical story we are actively living in right now—portable temples going out to carry His presence all over the world. We become portable meeting places where those who are still exiled from God can meet Him, through us. This is amazing, but something even better is coming. A new garden.

A NEW GARDEN AND THE NEW JERUSALEM (REVELATION 21)

After Jesus left, He sent His Spirit to dwell within us. He gave us a mission to share with others the good news that friendship with God is possible, by faith in Jesus Christ.

We don't know how long this period of time will last. But a day is coming when Jesus will return and make all things right. Jesus is coming back to finally eradicate all evil and death from the world and establish a new garden.

When Jesus returns and is victorious over evil, then heaven and earth will be remade into a new heaven and new earth joined together. At the very end of the Bible, in Revelation 21, we see a description of this new garden. A new Jerusalem comes down out of heaven to join earth.

What does this mean? The Bible explains, "Behold the dwelling place of God is with man. He will dwell with them, and they will be his people, and God himself will be with them as their God. He will wipe away every tear from their eyes, and death shall be no more, neither shall there be mourning, nor crying, nor pain anymore, for the former things have passed away" (Revelation 21:3–4).

Did you see it? The three-fold covenant goal of God from way back in the wilderness is finally realized. He says, in the end,

- – I will be your God,
- – you will be My people,
- – and I will dwell with you, forever and ever.

And this will be a perfect dwelling place. No sorrow. No pain. No death. No miscommunication. No fig leaves. No hiding. No temptation. Only pure friendship and intimacy with God and each other. Forever. We will be with Him, in a garden, forever.

In the last chapter of the Bible, we read about this new garden. There's a river flowing from the throne of God right through the new Jerusalem city. It's a garden city. And next to this river is a tree. You guessed it—this is the Tree of Life from way back in Genesis. We will have access to eternal life, but this time with no fear, no sin, no shame, and no death. Only friendship with God. Friendship, intimacy, and walking with God, forever, in the cool of the day. I cannot wait.

That's the story of the Bible. Friendship with God. Dwelling with God.

You may be wondering, *Now what? If all this is true, what do I practically do now? Does the Bible give any hints or suggestions on how to encounter and experience this glorious God—today?*

Yes, it does. That's what we will look at in the next chapter.

Chapter Three

SEEKING HIS PRESENCE

You will seek me and find me, when you
seek me with all your heart.

– Jeremiah 29:13

In the last chapter, we looked at the extraordinary lengths God has gone through to be with us. He is after you and wants to be with you, today. So, what do we need to do?

Here's what we are to do: seek Him.

But it's important to have the last chapter in mind. Seeking God is not a cosmic game of hide-and-seek. God is not hiding; rather, He is wooing. You can seek Him because He is waiting to be found and ready to be with you.

COMMANDED TO SEEK HIM

Psalm 105:4 says, "Seek the LORD and his strength; seek his presence continually!"

The word *seek* means to intentionally search for something that one desires. It is an active word that encourages us to intentionally go after something or someone. It's also a command in Scripture. We are commanded to seek after something. The Bible is saying, "Don't sit around and wait for something to come to you. Go get it."

It's a little like when you've lost your keys and are late for work.

There's an intensity to your searching, isn't there? You have an obsessive focus on finding the keys. Nothing matters except finding the keys. You are blind to anything else. You scream at your spouse and kids, "Where are the keys?"

And what happens when you find them? Joy! Cheering! Telling everyone around you, "I found them!" That is the flavor of this command in Scripture.

But what are we seeking exactly? What are we supposed to be searching for?

His presence.

The Hebrew word for *presence* means "face." We are commanded to seek the face of God. The term *face* implies relational intimacy. God's presence isn't simply an abstract thing or feeling or energy. His presence is His face. His presence is *Him*. You are commanded to seek *Him*.

But that's not all.

CONTINUAL SEEKING

The command is to seek His face "continually." That word, *continually*, is interesting in the Old Testament. It refers to an ongoing activity that is either constant or regularly scheduled.

The imagery and usage of this Hebrew word pictures the daily offerings and activities occurring in the temple. For example, in Exodus 29:38, God gives instructions about the daily sacrifices saying, "This is what you shall offer on the altar: two lambs a year old day by day regularly." That last word, "regularly," is the same word used in the psalm that says to seek His face continually. Another example is in Leviticus 6:13: "Fire shall be kept burning on the altar continually; it shall not go out." This is the language of worship and presence.

The people made offerings regularly, each day. The fire on the altar was burning continually, all day long. So, follow me on this: seeking God's face is a regular activity that is ongoing in our lives. We are commanded to seek God and His presence all the time, just like the regular, daily offerings made in the temple.

Our seeking after God's face is to burn continually and not go out. That may sound intense. And, frankly, it is. If I'm honest about my own heart and desires, I don't feel that way about God—not all the time. I don't burn with desire for God's face and presence all the time, continually, 24-7. I don't experience continual worship and enjoyment of Him all the time. I pray that I would, and I am growing in this lifestyle of worship and enjoyment, but I am not there yet.

I imagine the same is true for you.

Well, then, what do we do with that? Is the Bible untrue? Should we ignore this command because it seems difficult? Is this a dramatic and super-intense idea I can smile and nod at but not take seriously?

That would be the easy thing to do, but it would be costly. Let me explain.

WHY SEEK HIM?

Why should we seek God? This is actually a big question. Why should we seek after the face of God with that kind of intensity and ongoing passion? Why search for Him like my lost keys—blinded from everything else until we get Him?

The short answer is *selfishness*.

Now stick with me, here. We all naturally seek what we really want deep down. Consider the concept of hunger. When a baby is hungry, what does the baby do? Cries until he or she gets food. When my wife and kids get "hangry," what do I need to do? Get them food.

Every one of us has an intentional and ongoing rhythm of satisfying our hunger by eating food. We don't have to be commanded to do it, right? We get hungry, so we seek after food to eat. Simple.

In this way, we are naturally selfish, and no one gets blamed for this. We eat food because if we don't eat, we die. We get thirsty and selfishly seek after water because if we don't drink water, we die. Simple.

Here's the deal. The presence of God *is* life. Without Him we are starving and thirsty, spiritually speaking. Only God can satisfy the hunger and thirst of our hearts.

Consider the following psalms:

As a deer pants for flowing streams, so pants my soul for you, O God. My soul thirsts for God, for the living God. (Psalm 42:1–2)

O God, you are my God; earnestly I seek you; my soul thirsts for you; my flesh faints for you, as in a dry and weary land where there is no water. (Psalm 63:1)

I stretch out my hands to you; my soul thirsts for you like a parched land. (Psalm 143:6)

What is the psalmist saying here? He is saying, "I need God like I need water and food. If I don't experience His face and presence, I am starving and on my way to death. I need You, God!"

We are all selfish. We all intentionally seek the things we need for life and happiness. Bottom line: the only person who will satisfy you and bring you true joy is God Himself.

C. S. Lewis explains, "It would seem that Our Lord finds our desires not too strong, but too weak. We are half-hearted creatures, fooling about with drink and sex and ambition when infinite joy is offered us, like an ignorant child who wants to go on making mud pies in a slum because he cannot imagine what is meant by the offer of a holiday at the sea. We are far too easily pleased."[1]

Psalm 16:11 says, "You make known to me the path of life; in your presence there is fullness of joy; at your right hand are pleasures forevermore." The presence of God—His face—is full joy. That's what the Bible says. He has life. He *is* life. He has joy. He *is* joy. Being with Him is life and joy! What your heart wants more than anything else is found in God's presence. Life. Joy. Peace. Purpose. Love. Forgiveness. Wholeness. You will only find those things in Him! Let me illustrate this in a story. This is a story Jesus told many years ago.

FULL JOY IN HIS PRESENCE

There was a wealthy businessman who had two sons. The older son was mature and conscientious and a little judgmental. The younger son was wild and impulsive. One day, the younger son told his dad, "I'm done with this family and the family business. You guys are boring. Dad, I wish you were dead, so I could be free from you. Give me my share of the business, because I'm taking off to do what I want, with whoever I want, whenever I want."

So the younger son took his dad's money and went off to Vegas. He did exactly what he wanted to do—everything his heart desired. After a little while, he burned through the money, and it was all gone. He got kicked out of his hotel room and was homeless, eating trash from the casino alleyway.

Then he came to his senses.

He remembered his family and his father back home. He thought to himself, Maybe Dad will forgive me and take me back as an employee in the business. I'll never be a part owner again, but at least as an employee I'll have food and a place to stay.

He rehearsed his confession and apology as he hitchhiked his way back home. When he stepped onto the long driveway entrance of his family's house, he was preparing his speech. Consumed in thought, the son was unaware that his father was sitting on the porch.

When the father saw his son, still muttering his rehearsed speech under his breath, the father sprinted barefoot with joy. This father, who had been rejected, hated, and exploited, had one thought on his mind: *there's my boy and I want him back.*

When the father reached him, the son began his rehearsed apology-speech. But before he could finish, the father silenced him with kisses and an embrace. He held his son's face in his hands and wept for joy. His son was lost, but now he was found.

The younger son was fully restored to his status as part owner in the business. His dad had a new suit and shoes made for him to wear. Then they had a party and ate together. The son had been lost, but now he was back home with his father.

COMING TO YOUR SENSES

This story, originally told by Jesus, gives us some clues about selfishly seeking our joy in God. The businessman-father is God. The younger son is you and me. We think we know what we want, and it's not God or His presence. We want everything else but Him. We want the fruit from the tree in the garden, so we run away from God and find ourselves hungry. We eat and drink and partake of so many different things. For a while they might even be satisfying, but it never lasts.

This is the cycle of sin. We look away from God—who is life and joy—and think we are going to be satisfied by lesser joys. They eventually leave us hungrier and more broken and filled with more shame.

So, we hide from God, ashamed, and look for more things to satisfy us. This is addiction. For a time, I was addicted to porn. I thought that looking at images on my computer screen would satisfy the longing for love inside my heart. It felt good for a little bit, but afterward I felt even emptier. I felt more broken and had more shame than before.

This cycle is deadly. We feel emptiness and shame, so we eat the fruit of sin. This produces even greater shame, which we then try to fill with even more fruit of sin. This addiction cycle of shame, sin, and brokenness will destroy you and those around you.

This is the enemy's plan against you right now: to steal life from you. He will tempt you with lesser joys and seek to destroy you in a cycle of shame, sin, and hiding from God. The enemy will do anything He can to convince you that the presence and face of God will not satisfy you. He will try to convince you that you don't have time to seek the presence of God in your daily life—or that it's too hard or too boring.

The enemy will present shiny objects to distract you from the one thing that will bring life and joy to your life. The enemy hates you. The enemy hates God. And he really hates it when you and I stop hiding from God and seek after Him for joy and life.

The key moment in the story is when the younger son *comes to his senses*. He looks around and says, "Where am I?" He's in an alleyway eating trash and realizes that he's dying. He reasons that his dad is gracious and will give him what he needs to survive. So, he drops the trash-fruit in his hand, gets up, and goes to his dad.

For me, this meant coming to my senses and realizing that pornography didn't satisfy me but instead was destroying me on the inside. I would put the trash-fruit down, step away from the computer, and go to the Father with my confession.

It wasn't easy. For quite a while, I didn't understand radical grace, and I was thinking like this younger son, who rehearsed his confession, hoping for the best. The best he could imagine was an "employee" relationship with his dad, not one that was fully restored to family intimacy.

Similarly, for a long time I would confess and then feel that I needed to be in a probation period with God. This usually included lots of time praying and reading the Bible and being "good" for a while before He would *really* forgive me. Then after a day or two, I would "feel" like He forgave me. But by that time, temptation was back, and I would get caught in the cycle of shame and sin again.

Then one day I read this story and saw the perspective of the Father with His son. The Father didn't even wait for the full confession from the son before He forgave him! He didn't require a probationary period but accepted His son completely—as if he had never left.

Jesus showed me that this is the way the Father is with me when I confess and turn back to Him. Jesus paid for my sin on the cross and provided access for me back into a restored relationship with the Father. I don't need to add anything to the payment Jesus made for me!

This is radical grace. I still shake my head at this truth. It's too good. Jesus died in my place for my porn addiction and gave me His innocence. My addiction is credited to Jesus on the cross and His righteousness is credited to me in the eyes of the Father. Jesus became my sin so that I would become His righteousness (2 Corinthians 5:21)! This is *amazing grace*!

THE SAME IS TRUE FOR YOU

You are seeking something right now to satisfy you. Is it the Father or something else? Or someone else? Take it from me, lesser joys may feel good for a time, but eventually you will come crashing back down to emptiness and brokenness. So, put that trash-fruit down. Come to your senses. Get up and go to the Father, by faith in Jesus' death on the cross for your sin. Run to the Father. Confess your sin. Receive forgiveness and grace. Be clothed with the Spirit of God. Be restored to joy.

We are all seeking what we think will satisfy us. We are all seeking life, joy, peace, and purpose. The truth is you can choose to seek after the Father's face in Jesus—or not. If you run after those other things, they may be good for a little while, but they will not ultimately satisfy. So, be selfish. Seek the one thing that will actually bring you joy and life—the Father. He is waiting.

Take a minute right now. Close your eyes and picture Jesus. Hand him the trash-fruit you've been eating and seeking. Confess your sin and shame. Ask Him to forgive you and bring you back to the Father. Then receive the Father's embrace. Receive His joy. Receive His tears as they wash away the smeared stains of guilt, shame, brokenness, and sin.

It is here, forgiven and loved, that we enjoy the presence of the Father. This is life—with Him. This is joy—His face. This is what you have been longing for—the joy of the Father's presence.

This radical grace is the soil for friendship and intimacy with God the Father. To grow in friendship with the Father, we need to give time to Him, have conversation with Him, and do things together.

In the next section, we will explore the first ingredient: how to intentionally practice the Father's presence in your life. If you want to be friends with God, you must spend time in His presence. You must learn how to say, "Here I am."

Part Two

HERE I AM

Now Moses was keeping the flock of his father-in-law, Jethro, the priest of Midian, and he led his flock to the west side of the wilderness and came to Horeb, the mountain of God.

And the angel of the LORD appeared to him in a flame of fire out of the midst of a bush. He looked, and behold, the bush was burning, yet it was not consumed. And Moses said, "I will turn aside to see this great sight, why the bush is not burned."

When the LORD saw that he turned aside to see, God called to him out of the bush, "Moses, Moses!" And he said, "Here I am."

Then he said, "Do not come near; take your sandals off your feet, for the place on which you are standing is holy ground."

– Exodus 3:1–5

Chapter Four

SHOW ME
YOUR GLORY

"If your presence will not go with me, do not bring us up
from here. . . . Please show me your glory."
– Exodus 33:15, 18

From the very first time I read the story of Moses, I was challenged. I was confronted with a man hungry for the presence of God in a way I wasn't. I felt challenged and a little defeated. There's no way I could be like that. I'm just Jamie, not some great man of God.

But over the last several years, the Father has changed my thinking. Moses is not greater than you or me. In fact, Jesus said that in the new covenant, even the least of us is greater than the heroes of the old covenant (Luke 7:28). Why is that? Because the new covenant is better than the old. In the old covenant there was daily sacrifice for sin, but in the new covenant there is one sacrifice, and His name is Jesus. In the old covenant, the presence of God was available to a few, at a distance, but in the new, we get the Father's presence within all of us. It's positively amazing, and it's because of Jesus.

You see, Jesus is the mediator who brings us into relationship with the Father. He is the One who said, "Here I Am! I will go rescue My people from their slavery to their own sin." Jesus provides us access to His glory and presence. He is the hero of the story.

Moses is a shadow of what Jesus came to accomplish. Moses had a destiny to set his brothers and sisters free from slavery in Egypt; Jesus came to set the world free from slavery to sin and death. Moses met with God face-to-face as a representative for the people of God; Jesus is the face of God, who meets with us. The people watched Moses meet with God face-to-face, and vicariously experienced that friendship; Jesus is willing and ready to meet with all of us, anytime, all the time.

FACE-TO-FACE FRIENDSHIP

Why am I saying all this? Because you, reader, may be tempted to think that only Moses gets this kind of face-to-face relationship with God. Or you might be tempted to think that only the pastor of your church could have this kind of relationship with God. Or that I, as the author, have special access to God because I wrote a book on the subject. But all that is just enemy interference.

Hear me clearly: the Father wants face-to-face friendship with you, right now.

But how do we seek the Father's presence continually? How, practically, do we do this? What do we need to do to experience the Father face-to-face? To experience His glory and presence? The goal of this chapter is to be practical and helpful to you. We will use Moses as a model and pull out some helpful principles for practicing God's presence in your daily life.

Stop Disqualifying Yourself

First, stop disqualifying yourself. Did you know that Moses was eighty years old before he encountered God? It's never too late to start. You can encounter the Father right now, whether you are eight or eighty. If you've never heard His voice or experienced Him, you can today.

Also, did you know that Moses was a failed leader? He had a destiny from God to rescue his Israelite family from slavery in Egypt, and he blew it. He killed an Egyptian, then tried to cover it up. That was at age forty.

Moses got scared and ran off into the wilderness, ending up tending his father-in-law's sheep as an outcast, an outlaw, a failure. For forty years he tended sheep on the backside of nowhere. Alone. Hardly a leader of anyone, except smelly sheep.

Then God spoke to him from a burning bush, and everything changed—not because Moses did anything but because God chose to speak and encounter him. Moses was a failure, but that didn't deter the Father from meeting with him.

The same is true for you. You may think, *I've tried and failed so many times. I don't feel worthy. I'm washed up.* The truth is, we are all washed up. Seriously. Stop disqualifying yourself. The Father has a burning-bush moment for you. It could be this book you're reading.

Be Willing to Break Your Routine

Second, be willing to break your routine. For forty years, Moses traversed the same paths with the same sheep at the same time. Over and over. Routine. It makes us feel comfortable to have rhythm and routine. But something happened that broke his routine. Moses saw a bush on fire but not consumed. He said to himself, "Huh, that's weird. I wonder what's going on. I'll go check it out."

Moses had a path and routine that he took every day with the sheep. But he chose to break that routine to see something—a burning bush—that caught his eye. The Bible says that "when the LORD saw that he turned aside to see, God called to him out of the bush" (Exodus 3:4).

Let me make this simple. Sometimes we miss what God is doing because we are unwilling to break our routine and look at what is happening around us. If you haven't been experiencing the presence of God in your daily life, it may be time to break your routine. It's time to break out of "autopilot" living and seek after the presence of God.

What if Moses hadn't stopped that day? What if he was more focused on getting the sheep watered? Now, there's nothing wrong with being responsible. It's a good thing to be responsible. But sometimes we can take it to the extreme and miss God.

How many times has the Father been trying to get your attention and you were too busy being responsible? Or in my case distracted by my phone. How many moments have I missed with God because I was distracted and busy and didn't have time on my schedule?

Be willing to break routine. Be on the lookout today. The Father has plans to break into your routine—today. Will you see Him? Will you see His face?

Say, "Here I Am"

Third, tell the Father, "Here I am." Don't underestimate these words. Be present with the Father. After Moses heard God call out his name, he responded, "Here I am." The rest is history . . . literally. The most significant event in Jewish history—Israel leaving slavery in Egypt—occurred because one man said, "Here I am," to God. This is no little thing I'm talking about. You and I miss out on so much that the Father has planned for us because we don't stop and say, "Here I am, Father. I am present to be with You."

The simple practice of stopping and saying "Here I am" will change your life. It changed Moses's life and, consequently, the people of Israel. An entire generation was set free because one man, a washed-up failure, said, "Here I am," to God.

When you get up in the morning and your eyes open, don't pick up your phone and check what everyone else is saying. First, when you open your eyes, say, "Here I am, Father. I'm ready to experience this day with you." Then, after you make coffee and are preparing for your day, tell Him again, "Here I am, Father. What do you think about my schedule today?"

Be present with Him. He will change your life. Mindfulness and living present with the Father will do that—I promise. Consider setting an alarm to go off regularly throughout the day. This is a simple practice to wake us out of those autopilot moments. Right now, I have my iPhone alarm set to go off once an hour, all day. When I hear the alarm, I am reminded to be present with the Father.

Of course, God is always with us. That's true. Theology tells us that God is *omnipresent*. He is present everywhere, and He is always present. But we are not always aware of His presence with us. Many days, we live our lives ignoring Him. I know I do. I have gone days at a time and never considered that the Father is present with me all day.

So, the simple practice of setting an alarm on my phone forces me to seek His face every hour. You don't have to set it for every hour; you can set it more frequently, say, every thirty minutes. Or you may choose to set an alarm for every two or three hours. The importance of this practice is not about frequency but mindfulness of His presence during the day.

Don't live on autopilot. Be willing to break routine and see where God's presence will lead you. There are burning-bush moments available today for you. Will you see them? Will you stop and experience His presence today?

Ask for More of Him

Fourth, ask for more. Ask the Father for more of His presence and glory in your life. Skipping ahead in the story, we see another interaction between Moses and God. After the exodus from Egypt, Moses asks God, "Show me Your glory." He wanted more.

Moses had seen plagues, miracles, signs, and wonders. He saw the parting of the sea, the destruction of Pharaoh's army, and God writing the Ten Commandments. He spent forty days on Mount Sinai. But Moses is still not satisfied. He wants more of God. He desires more of God's presence.

After all that Moses has seen and experienced of God, he asks for more. The man described as "a friend of God" and who spoke "face-to-face" with the Creator of the universe wants more of Him.

I am too easily satisfied with yesterday's experience of God. How about you?

We can experience more of God, and we are encouraged to ask for more. More intimacy with the Father is available. More friendship with Jesus is available. More of the Holy Spirit's presence is available.

This is about hunger. This is what seeking the Father's presence continually looks like—hunger for more. Are you hungry for more of Him?

Do you think there's more you could learn about the Creator of the universe? Of course! He is the glorious One. He is the King. He is the Beginning and the End. He is the Creator and Redeemer of all things. He is inexhaustible in His glory, and He is willing to give you more of Himself; you just need to ask Him for more.

A. W. Tozer said, "You have as much of God as you actually want." That's the heart behind Moses's cry to God: "Show me Your glory."[2]

I want as much of the Father, Son, and Holy Spirit as I can handle today. I want to learn more about His glory and power and purposes for my life and for my family. I want more of Him today than I experienced yesterday. Tomorrow, and next week, and the next, give me even more. And I want that for you too. This can be a burning-bush moment for you right now. Tell the Father, "Here I am, present with You. Show me Your glory." Seek Him.

By the way, if you think this is over the top, consider this: we will not stop learning and experiencing more of the Father for all eternity. After two millennia of experiencing more and more of His glory, there will be still more to learn.

Remember Tozer's quote, "You have as much of God as you actually want." Your current enjoyment of God's presence is entirely up to you, my friend. If you want more of Him, then ask Him for more.

Follow His Glory and Presence

Finally, follow His glory and presence daily. At the end of the book of Exodus, there is a summary statement about the way the people of Israel interacted with God in the wilderness:

> Throughout all their journeys, whenever the cloud was taken up from over the tabernacle, the people of Israel would set out. But if the cloud was not taken up, then they did not set out till the day that it was taken up. For the cloud of the Lord was on the tabernacle by day, and fire was in it by night, in the sight of all the house of Israel throughout all their journeys. (Exodus 40:36–38)

The people of God learned dependence on Him every day. God's glory was over the tabernacle as a cloud during the day and as a fire at night. When the glory lifted from the tabernacle, they packed up camp and prepared to follow Him. When God's glory stayed put, they stayed put. Simple. Every day they followed the glory and presence of God. Their daily life was oriented to the presence of God. Their coming and going was in relation to whether God was coming or going.

Earlier in the story, Moses expressed this to God: "If your presence will not go with me, do not bring us up from here" (Exodus 33:15). Moses's job was to lead the people of Israel. He understood that he and the people needed God's presence more than anything else. He wasn't moving the people if the presence of God wasn't going with them.

What about you? When you walk into your staff meeting at work, do you acknowledge your need for God's presence? Are you aware that you can put your hand to something—like your job, family, or ministry work—and not have the favor and blessing of God upon it? It is entirely possible to spend all day doing your tasks without the Father's presence. Your life can be built in vain if it's not built with the presence of the Father.

As you grow in friendship with God, you will develop sensitivity to following Him in everything you do. Try it today. Whatever is on your schedule for today, ask the Father to manifest His glory and presence on that activity. He will either bless it or not. I want to put my hands to things that He has scheduled and blessed with His presence. How about you?

I'm not suggesting you abandon your responsibilities and wait for God to lead you in every decision. This will lead to paralysis. No, I am suggesting that your daily schedule needs to have His presence within it. Ask Him to go with you, and then accomplish your tasks for the day. His presence may lift from an activity. This will provide an opportunity to stop, break routine, be present with Him, and ask Him to show His glory to you. Be present. He will show you the way.

EFFECTS OF INTENTIONAL MINDFULNESS OF GOD'S PRESENCE

Let's close with a couple of examples of the effects of practicing God's presence in daily life. What will happen to you if you intentionally seek His face every day?

First, you will change. The presence of God will change you, and this will be obvious to those around you. When Moses came down from Mount Sinai, the Bible says that his face was shining "because he had been talking with God" (Exodus 34:29). Regular and intentional seeking of God's glory changed Moses, and everyone could see the change. His face was visibly shining because Moses had been with God. He looked different because of the presence of God.

I want to look and smell like the Father to those around me. I desire to be so intentional about seeking God's presence daily that others encounter Him by being near me. What if you practiced "Here I am" with God so regularly in the mornings that those around you could smell the spiritual aroma of Jesus on you? We as believers should look different from the world because of the presence of God. We should have the fragrance of Christ. You want a simple practice to transform your life? Stay in the presence of God.

Second, those around you will be transformed too. All the people led by Moses experienced blessing from his regular practice of God's presence. They were being changed because their leader was being changed. Do not underestimate the transformation that is available to those around you when you intentionally practice daily mindfulness toward God.

There was one person in Moses's life who was profoundly altered by God's presence: Joshua. The Bible records that Moses would regularly talk to God and see Him face-to-face, like a friend. When Moses would leave to go speak with the people, his assistant, Joshua, "would not depart from the tent" (Exodus 33:11).

This young protégé of Moses stayed in the presence of God and would not leave God's presence. Joshua learned from his mentor the value of God's presence, and he stayed in the tent. He learned how to practice the presence of God as a young man. Joshua would become the new leader of Israel—having learned the importance of God's presence, Joshua would lead the people into the promised land.

The church in North America is hemorrhaging young people. Young men and women who grew up in the church are leaving the faith of their fathers and mothers. An entire generation is walking away from God. Our strategy to keep these young people can no longer consist of entertainment and cute, "relevant" programs. We must show them, again, the value and glory of God's presence. Our own intentional practice of God's presence will model to them what real Christianity looks like.

It is our responsibility to say "Here I am" to God every day. He will change us as we ask Him for more and more of His glory in our lives. We will be changed, but the next generation will be changed too. They will become hungry for more of God's glory because they have seen that same hunger modeled by us. "Father, show us your glory!" Do this for our sake and for the sake of the next generation.

There is another effect of intentionally seeking the presence of God: peace. In the next chapter, we will explore the power of God's presence when we are afraid.

Chapter Five

THE HIDING
PLACE

God is our refuge and strength, a very present help in
trouble. Therefore we will not fear.

– Psalm 46:1–2

I'm a Texas boy, and I married an Oklahoma girl. Growing up, we both experienced regular tornado drills in our elementary schools. Tornadoes are a reality for these areas of the country, especially in Oklahoma.

For five years, we lived in Tulsa. I pastored a church, and Jess directed a state-wide, nonprofit program that helps at-risk kids and their families. During these years, we had several close calls with tornadoes.

While at church one Wednesday night, a tornado formed and began to head straight toward our house. We watched on the news as it jumped over our neighborhood and landed near our kids' elementary school. Several surrounding homes were damaged.

On another occasion, Jess's work building was struck by a tornado and, thankfully, sustained only minor window damage. Unfortunately, the office building across the street was so damaged it is still vacant. That building has never recovered.

You learn something about tornadoes when they are regular visitors to your part of the country. You learn that there are early warning signs before a tornado strikes. For example, when the sky turns green, you know something is up. Also, when the birds scatter and it gets quiet, something is coming, and it's probably not good.

Thanks to technology, when you hear the sirens go off, that means it's time to take cover in what Jess affectionately calls "hidey holes." These are storm shelters you should immediately seek out once you hear the warning sirens. They are designed to protect you from debris and the tornado itself. When a tornado hits, you want to be in the shelter. And it helps to know the warning signs that something is up.

EARLY WARNING SYSTEM

I've learned to identify one of the most important warning signs in my own heart: anxiety. This has been one of the most difficult lessons I've ever learned in my life. And I'm still learning it today.

Here's the lesson: when I'm anxious, that is an early warning sign that I need to find shelter fast. For me, anxiety usually occurs when I'm thinking about something that might happen in the future. I've convinced myself that some event or experience is going to be bad, hurtful, or difficult. Worry creeps in, and I will begin to obsess about what *might* happen. What I'm learning is that this anxiety is a sign that I'm not living in the present. Instead, I'm worried about what might happen in the future.

Here's the big idea for this chapter: as soon as anxiety hits you, find the shelter. When those creeping thoughts begin to crowd your mind, run to your hiding place. Find the "hidey hole" where you will find rest and protection from the debris and the storm.

YOU ARE A HIDING PLACE FOR ME

The psalmists write in many places about this shelter. Here are just a few:

> He who dwells in the shelter of the Most High
>   will abide in the shadow of the Almighty.
> I will say to the LORD, "My refuge and my fortress,
>   my God, in whom I trust." (Psalm 91:1–2)
>
> You are a hiding place for me;
>   you preserve me from trouble;

you surround me with shouts of de-
liverance. (Psalm 32:7)

In the cover of your presence you hide them
    from the plots of men;
you store them in your shelter
    from the strife of tongues. (Psalm 31:20)

You are my hiding place and my shield. (Psalm 119:114)

God is our refuge and strength,
    a very present help in trouble.
Therefore we will not fear. (Psalm 46:1–2)

In the psalms, we are encouraged by the experiences of these worshipers. David and others found shelter in God. He was their hiding place. He was their refuge and strong fortress. God's presence hid
them from danger. The presence of God was a refuge and strength in
times of trouble.

I've discovered that when anxiety hits, it's time to immediately take
cover in the shelter and presence of God. His presence *is* the hiding
place. This chapter is about how we do that practically. How do you
rest in the shadow of the Almighty? How do you hide in His presence?

PEACE IS A PERSON

Well, first let's make this concept concrete. Peace is not found in a
place or in your circumstances. Peace is found in a person. In fact,
peace *is* a person, a person named Jesus. One of His royal titles is
Prince of Peace (Isaiah 9:6). Do you think He might know a thing or
two about countering fear and anxiety? Sure. He is the King of peace.
Jesus is peace.

When His disciples were experiencing fear in the middle of a raging
windstorm on the Sea of Galilee, where was Jesus? What was the Prince
of Peace doing? He was asleep. Their boat was filling up with water,
and the disciples—most of whom were experienced fishermen—were
legitimately afraid. Yet they found Jesus asleep on the bottom of the
boat.

Here's the truth: Jesus is not stressed or worried about anything. He
is completely at peace. The disciples wake Him up, wondering if He

even cares about what they're going through? "Don't you care, Jesus? We are dying here!"

He got up, calmed the storm, turned to His disciples, and replied, "Where is your faith?" (Matthew 8:23–27; Mark 4:35–41; Luke 8:22–25).

Faith. There it is. But what is faith?

Faith is trusting Jesus more than whatever you're worried about—that thing that might happen in the future. Faith is resting "present tense" with Jesus. Remember, He is not stressed. But worry is your mind scurrying "future tense" to what *might* be. Faith is being present with Jesus, even in the storms of your life. Faith is noticing the early warning signs of fear and going directly to the shelter, which is Jesus. He is your hiding place. Jesus is your refuge and strength.

DAVID STRENGTHENED HIMSELF IN THE LORD

The great psalmist and king, David, was known for his courage and bravery in battle. He fought lions and giants and bears! He defeated powerful enemies, both at home and abroad. He was a leader of mighty men and warriors. But where did all that bravery come from? Have you ever thought about that?

There's a fascinating moment in the life of David I want you to see. The story is in 1 Samuel 30, and it sheds light on David's mindset when he pens these Psalm passages about refuge and strength. Here's the setup. David has been at war with the enemy, the Amalekites, with his mighty men and other warriors. While they were out fighting, the enemy backtracked and attacked David's home base at Ziklag, burned down the city, and took all their wives and children. When David and his warriors found out what happened, they wept until all their strength was gone.

They lost their homes. They lost their wives. They lost their children. Can you imagine the fear and anxiety? Would they ever see their loved ones again? What are the enemy forces doing to their wives and kids? What has happened to them?

The Bible records, "David was greatly distressed, for the people spoke of stoning him, because all the people were bitter in soul, each for his sons and daughters" (1 Samuel 30:6). The word *distressed* here means to be in trouble and marked by anxious uneasiness. David is worried, troubled, and wondering if he will even survive this ordeal.

Ever been there? Yep, me too.

So, what does David do? Remember, this is the same guy who wrote those words *fortress*, *hiding place*, and *shelter*. Will he practice what he preached in the psalms that he wrote? Absolutely.

Here's what the Bible says happened next: "David was greatly distressed, . . . But [he] strengthened himself in the LORD his God" (1 Samuel 30:6). David sought the Lord, not his circumstances, for strength. The situation looked bleak for his family and even his own life. Where did he go? He went straight to his fortress for strength.

Remember Psalm 105:4 from chapter 3? The psalmist says, "Seek the LORD and his strength; seek his presence continually!" Earlier we looked at the second half of that verse, "Seek his presence." The first half says the same thing but in a different way. This is a literary form called parallelism. Instead of the command to seek His presence, the parallel is "Seek the Lord and his *strength*" (emphasis mine). Seeking the presence of God looks like seeking Him and His strength, especially when you are anxious or afraid.

I LOVE YOU, O LORD, MY STRENGTH

What might that have looked like in David's heart? Well, here's what David wrote when he was delivered on another occasion: "I love you, O LORD, my strength. The LORD is my rock and my fortress and my deliverer, my God, my rock, in whom I take refuge, my shield, and the horn of my salvation, my stronghold. I call upon the LORD, who is worthy to be praised, and I am saved from my enemies" (Psalm 18:1–3).

When confronted with fear and anxiety, David runs straight to his refuge and strength—God Himself. He wasn't going to find comfort or support from anyone else because all those around him were thinking murderous thoughts. David could only go to one place, the hiding place in the presence of God.

The rest of the story goes like this: David strengthened himself in the "LORD *his God*" (1 Samuel 30:6, emphasis mine). I love that. There's history and intimacy between David and God. They've spent years together, out in the fields with the sheep. David and his God. After strengthening himself, David called in the priest and inquired of the Lord as to what he should do. The Lord told him to go get his family back, so David took off, chased down the Amalekites, defeated them, and retrieved every one of the wives, kids, and livestock.

David knew where to go when he was anxious. He went directly to his "hidey hole" in the presence of God. The presence of God was David's hiding place. And God will be your hiding place too. Here are some practical steps to deal with fear and anxiety by practicing the presence of God, your strength.

PRACTICAL STEPS

1. Understand you will have legitimate distress in this world, but Jesus' peace is stronger. Jesus explained to His disciples, "In this world you will have trouble. But take heart! I have over-come the world" (John 16:33 NIV).

   There is nothing Pollyanna about Jesus. He doesn't come to you and say, "Follow Me, and you will never struggle in life again." No, Jesus is honest. You will experience distress. You will experience pain and suffering. You will be confronted with things in life that will tempt you to fear. But Jesus is stronger.

   Like His disciples on the boat, you will experience legiti-mately dangerous circumstances in your life. Remember, Jesus is in the boat with you. He is present with you. Even when you walk through the valley of the shadow of death, Jesus is with you.

2. Live present tense with Jesus. Jesus *is* peace. Right now, He is at peace. He is not worried about anything happening in your life. He knows how everything will turn out. So, if you want to regularly experience peace, then live present tense with Je-sus. When you live and think future tense, you are concerned with what *might* happen. You will be tempted to be anxious about things that may or may not ever occur.

   The enemy has twisted me up so many times with this. My mind will spin with worry about something in the future, and then if it actually does occur, it's not nearly as bad as I thought. Maybe this has happened to you too.

I've wasted entire days of my life worried about something that never ended up happening. Those days were stolen from me, because I wasn't living present tense with Jesus in the moment. I ignored Him and allowed my mind to spin with future tense worry. Worry is meditation on something or someone other than Jesus.

3. Give your anxiety to Jesus, and receive His peace. You can regularly exchange your fear of the waves around you for His calm.

We are actually commanded to do this in Scripture: "Cast all your anxiety on him because he cares for you" (1 Peter 5:7 NIV). The verb *cast* means to throw responsibility for something onto someone else. This verse encourages you to give Jesus the responsibility for your anxiety and worry. Let Him handle it. Make Him responsible for it. You can stop carrying that anxiety around and throw it to Jesus because He can handle it.

But that's not all. He will give you something to replace your anxiety. He will give you *His* peace. In John 14:27 Jesus says, "Peace I leave with you; my peace I give to you. Not as the world gives do I give to you. Let not your hearts be troubled, neither let them be afraid." The "world" doesn't have the resources to experience true peace, but Jesus does. Have you noticed how much fear is present in our culture? The world doesn't have peace, and it cannot provide it to you. You must receive Jesus' peace. And He will give it to you in exchange for your fear. Trade that fear away for His peace.

Practically, what does that look like? When you are experiencing anxiety, close your eyes and picture Jesus. Thank Him for being present with you. Picture yourself handing over a backpack full of your anxieties to Jesus. Take the backpack of worries off your back, and toss it to Him. Take a deep breath and exhale slowly. Watch Jesus take responsibility for that backpack. Then extend your hands like a child receiving a gift, and breathe deeply. Receive Jesus' peace.

4. Finally, draw near to Jesus with thanksgiving and worship. Let me make this as simple as possible: when we fix our hearts and minds on Jesus in worship, all other fears fade away. A favorite hymn from my childhood goes like this:

> Turn your eyes upon Jesus,
> Look full in His wonderful face,
> And the things of earth will grow strangely dim,
> In the light of His glory and grace.

When you feel anxiety and fear creeping up on you, draw near to Jesus. Enter the hiding place through worship. Begin to thank Jesus for everything you can think of in your life. Tell Him out loud what you are thankful for. Counter anxiety with thankfulness.

Then begin to speak or sing the psalms or other worship songs. Worship is warfare against fear. Sing. Lift your heart to Jesus. Lift your hands to Jesus. Praise Him for His goodness and grace. Praise Him for His glory and holiness. Rejoice in Him! Call out to Him! Thank Him, even in the middle of the tornado, that He is your refuge and strength. Worship Him until the storms around you are calmed. Praise Him until the fears within you fade away. Worship is warfare against anxiety.

Choose to rejoice. Choose to be thankful. Choose to hide yourself in Jesus. Choose to think about Him and receive His thoughts about your situation. Jesus is present, and He is peace.

The apostle Paul writes about this. I encourage you to allow these words to wash over you right now as you read them:

> Rejoice in the Lord always; again I will say, rejoice. Let your reasonableness be known to everyone. The Lord is at hand; do not be anxious about anything, but in everything by prayer and supplication with thanksgiving let your requests be made known to God. And

the peace of God, which surpasses all understanding, will guard your hearts and your minds in Christ Jesus.

Finally, brothers, whatever is true, whatever is honorable, whatever is just, whatever is pure, whatever is lovely, whatever is commendable, if there is any excellence, if there is anything worthy of praise, think about these things. What you have learned and received and heard and seen in me—practice these things, and the God of peace will be with you. (Philippians 4:4–9)

When the tornado sirens screech, you must find shelter in the hiding place. When the storms of life are coming against you, go to the bottom of the boat where Jesus is, asleep. He is your peace. His presence is your hiding place.

There is one more important truth about practicing God's presence. Friendship with God *feels* like something. His presence feels like *home*. God doesn't only want to be present with you; rather, He wants to make His home with you, and that is what we will explore in the next chapter.

Chapter Six

HOME IS WHERE
THE SPIRIT IS

Jesus answered him, "If anyone loves me, he will keep
my word, and my Father will love him, and we will
come to him and make our home with him."

– John 14:23

God wants to dwell with you. Yes, you. His desire is to be with you and enjoy this day with you, right now.

God wants to dwell with you. That word *dwell* is a significant word in the Bible and in the history of God with humanity. He wants to dwell with us. We touched on this in chapter 2, but I want to help bring it home to your heart in this chapter.

GOD WANTS TO BE AT HOME WITH YOU

The Hebrew word for *dwell* means to live, inhabit, rest, settle down, stay, abide, make a home somewhere. When God says He wants to dwell with you, that means He wants to be at home with you. It's a big deal to Him. This is clear from the sweep of the biblical story. From Genesis to Revelation, God has been at work to dwell with His people. From the beginning to the end, His plan is to dwell with you, to make His home with you.

In the beginning, He created the garden as a place to dwell with us (Genesis 1–2). At the end of all things and when the dust settles, He will declare, "Behold, the dwelling place of God is with man. He will dwell with them, and they will be his people, and God himself will be with them as their God" (Revelation 21:3).

God made a covenant with the people of Israel after He rescued them from slavery. The covenant formula is: (1) I will be your God, (2) you will be My people, and (3) I will dwell with you. The physical manifestation of that dwelling place was the tabernacle. The tabernacle was a portable worship space where God's glory and presence could come down and be at home with His people.

Through the prophets, God promises to go a step further. He says, "I will put my law within them, and I will write it on their hearts. And I will be their God, and they shall be my people" (Jeremiah 31:33). What's He saying? God is promising a new covenant where He will dwell not in a portable worship space but in the hearts of His people. He wants to dwell within His people. He wants to put His glory and His presence inside of us.

So He comes in human form and dwells on earth. The Gospel of John records, "And the Word [Jesus] became flesh and dwelt among us, and we have seen his glory, glory as of the only Son from the Father, full of grace and truth" (John 1:14). Jesus came to dwell with us, and His glory and presence is now available to all.

Then Jesus says something remarkable to His disciples. Jesus explains that He is going to leave them and that the Holy Spirit will come to dwell with them and be in them. He connects the presence of the Holy Spirit with home by saying: "If anyone loves me, he will keep my word, and my Father will love him, and we will come to him and make our home with him" (John 14:23).

Did you catch that? Jesus and the Father want to make *you* their home. God wants to love you and be at home with you forever. And the practical way this works is that they send the Holy Spirit to dwell within believers. It's amazing! The God who spoke billions of galaxies into being wants to reside and make His home inside of you.

This is one of the most crucial things you must understand if you want to regularly practice the presence of God in your life.

He wants to be at home with you.

He wants to dwell with you.

He wants to live with you.

God doesn't want to be an add-on to your day. He wants to experience your day *with* you. He doesn't just want a twenty-four-minute "quiet time" in the morning. He wants all twenty-four hours of your day with you.

The Father wants to make His home inside you. The Son provides you access to this relationship. The Holy Spirit is the Father and the Son dwelling within you.

WHO IS THE HOLY SPIRIT?

So, at this point, there may be some strange images going through your head about the indwelling presence of God. One image might be of a *Star Wars*-esque "force" that empowers you to be one with the universe. Another may be of an *Alien*-like creature inside you waiting to burst out. Or maybe all this talk of the Holy Spirit makes you think of wildly charismatic Christians who sometimes do really strange things.

But Jesus explains exactly who the Holy Spirit is in John chapters 14 and 16. Let's look at what He has to say about the Holy Spirit. Jesus is explaining to His disciples that He's not going to be around much longer. He will be heading back to heaven to be with the Father. Obviously, this causes His disciples some anxiety, so much so that He says to them, "Let not your hearts be troubled" (John 14:1).

During the conversation, Jesus encourages His disciples by explaining to them that even though He is leaving soon, it will all be okay. Why? Because the Holy Spirit is coming. He says, "These things I have spoken to you while I am still with you. But the Helper, the Holy Spirit, whom the Father will send in my name, he will teach you all things and bring to your remembrance all that I have said to you" (John 14:25–26). In this section of Scripture, Jesus explains at least five things that are important to know about the Holy Spirit.

The Holy Spirit Is a Person

First, the Holy Spirit is a person. Jesus uses the personal pronoun *He* when referring to the Holy Spirit. So this helps us understand that the Holy Spirit is a person, not a thing. He is not an "it" or a "force" but a person. That means He feels and thinks. As a person, the Holy

Spirit wants to communicate and grow in relationship with you. You can grow in friendship with the Holy Spirit just like any other person in your life. It takes time, conversation, and doing things together. I'll speak more on that later.

The Holy Spirit Is God

Second, the Holy Spirit isn't just *any* person. He's also God. Jesus says that the Father will send "another Helper, to be with you forever" (John 14:16). By calling the Holy Spirit "another Helper," Jesus connects Him to God. Jesus is the Advocate and Helper (1 John 2:1), and the Holy Spirit is another just like Him. If Jesus is God, and the Holy Spirit is another Helper like Jesus, then the Holy Spirit is God.

This isn't the only time that this truth comes up in Scripture. For example, Paul says to the Corinthian church, "Do you not know that you are God's temple and that God's Spirit dwells in you?" (1 Corinthians 3:16). God's temple is where God resides. And since the Holy Spirit is God, wherever He dwells is God's sacred space. Do you consider yourself to be holy ground? If you are a temple of the living God, then wherever you go is a holy place because God goes with you. It's amazing!

The Holy Spirit Is a Helper

Third, the Holy Spirit is a *helper* for you. That word refers to a wide range of helping. God the Holy Spirit is given to you to encourage and comfort you. He is given to be an advocate and representative for you.

I had often struggled with feeling alone with my emotions. Sometimes it was hard for me to express what was happening on the inside, and this left me feeling unknown and misunderstood. Then the Father opened my eyes to the Comforter who is available in the Holy Spirit. I am never alone because the Creator of the universe who loves me dwells within me and is there to encourage and help me. The information I'm sharing in this chapter about the Holy Spirit has changed my life. When you feel alone, understand that God is available to you as a guide, a friend, an encourager, and a helper.

The Holy Spirit Is a Teacher

Fourth, the Holy Spirit is a teacher. Jesus says that the Holy Spirit will "teach you all things and bring to your remembrance all that I have said to you" (John 14:26). Later, in chapter 16, Jesus continues, "I still have many things to say to you, but you cannot bear them now. When the Spirit of truth comes, he will guide you into all the truth, for he will not speak on his own authority, but whatever he hears he will speak, and he will declare to you the things that are to come. He will glorify me, for he will take what is mine and declare it to you" (John 16:12–14).

I love this aspect of the Holy Spirit's personality. He is a teacher. He loves to teach us, specifically about the things that Jesus taught. Like all good teachers, the Holy Spirit understands that we are all at different grade levels and need specialized teaching plans. He knows where you are and what you can handle right now.

I've been amazed at the number of times I've read the same passage only to learn something new about God or myself on the 150th time. And if I'm open and listening, the Holy Spirit is willing to teach me something new on the 151st time too. He's awesome. He is a genius and is excited to teach you new things. Unfortunately, many of us ignore Him, as I did for many years. Not anymore. I love to learn, and the master teacher dwells within me! He will teach you too.

The Holy Spirit Is Home

Finally, the Holy Spirit is *home*. Jesus explains, "I will ask the Father, and he will give you another Helper, to be with you forever. . . . You know [the Holy Spirit], for he dwells with you and will be in you. I will not leave you as orphans; I will come to you" (John 14:16–18). Notice the family language here. Jesus, the Son, will ask the Father to send the Spirit to us. Forever. We will not be orphans, without a family; rather, we will be full members of God's family. We will join a family with the Father, Son, and Holy Spirit.

The doctrine of the Trinity is a mind-boggling truth. God is one God, but He is three distinct persons. Each person of the Trinity is fully God. Yet, there are not three Gods but one. The Father is fully God, the Son is fully God, and the Spirit is fully God. And there is only one God. If your mind hurts thinking about this, then you are starting to get the doctrine right.

But the important thing to know is this: from eternity past God has always existed. He never started being—He has always been. And He has always been a family of three. The concept of family isn't a construct of human thinking. Family isn't something God created when He fashioned Adam and Eve. No, family is eternal.

God has eternally existed in family: Father, Son, and Holy Spirit. And this family has been perfect, forever. Perfect love. Perfect communication. Perfect and mutual yielding to each other. Conversation. Security. Peace. *Home.*

What you want more than anything is to be at home with a perfect family. You and I long for a place of belonging, love, intimacy, togetherness, and wholeness. Deep down, that's what we all want. Actually, it's not just what you want. It's also what you were created by and for: family. You were created *by* a family—the triune God— and you were created *for* a family with Him, forever.

Look at what Jesus says: "I will not leave you as orphans." Then He follows that up with "If anyone loves me, he will keep my word, and my Father will love him, and we will come to him and make our home with him" (John 14:23). The Holy Spirit dwelling within you is home for the triune God. This eternal family—Father, Son, and Spirit— wants to be at home with you. You get to join in this perfect, eternal family, and you will never be kicked out!

How Do I Get Him?

The big question, then, is *How do I get into this family?* Some think we are automatically in God's family, but the truth is we must be *adopted.* Very simply, you and I are adopted by the Father, through the Spirit, by faith in Jesus.

The apostle Paul explains it this way, "But when the fullness of time had come, God sent forth his Son, born of woman, born under the law, to redeem those who were under the law, so that we might receive adoption as sons. And because you are sons, God has sent the Spirit of his Son into our hearts, crying, 'Abba! Father!'" (Galatians 4:4–6). What is Paul saying here? Adoption is available to us from the Father by faith in the Son. Jesus came to die on the cross for our sin and brokenness. His death and resurrection, on our behalf, provides us this adoption.

The process of adoption was common in the Roman world. Paul's audience, the Galatians, would have understood what he was saying to them. In Rome, adoptions could occur at any age. It wasn't just kids being adopted. Adults could be adopted too. The most famous adoption in Rome was Julius Caesar's adoption of Octavian to be his heir.

In a Roman adoption, the son's or daughter's previous identity, name, and debts were erased. The identification papers of their old life were torn up and discarded. The adopted son or daughter was defined completely by their relationship with the new father, whose wealth and status were now *their* inheritance and identity. This choice was graciously made by the adopting father because orphans didn't have the resources to buy this relationship. It was a free, gracious gift and act of love on behalf of the adopting father.

Paul was saying that the same is true when God adopts us. You can't purchase this adoption or relationship. You don't have enough money or good deeds to accomplish it. You can't buy your way into this family. Adoption is graciously given to you by faith in Jesus. When you put your trust in Jesus' death for your sins, you are adopted into the Father's family by the Holy Spirit.

By faith, your old life, identity, and sin are nailed to the cross with Jesus. He becomes your sin and gives you His righteousness. Your old identity is torn up and discarded. Now you are defined by the Father and your relationship with Him. His wealth and status are now your inheritance and identity. All this is freely given to you by the Father, through the Spirit, and by faith in the Son. The Holy Spirit is sent to make this truth "real" to you, deep down in your heart.

We see a picture of this truth at Jesus' baptism. When He came out of the water, two things happened. First, the Holy Spirit descended onto Jesus. Second, a voice came from heaven and said, "This is my beloved Son, with whom I am well pleased" (Matthew 3:16–17). At that moment, the Father was proudly declaring: "This is My beautiful Son. I love Him and am so proud of Him. That's My Boy!"

Here's the good news. By faith in Jesus, your new identity is exactly the same as His. You are gifted with the Holy Spirit dwelling within you. You receive the approval of the Father. What is true of Jesus is now true of you. You are the beloved son of the Father. You are the cherished daughter of the Father.

The Holy Spirit helps you understand this reality. By faith in Christ, you delight the Father. He is proud of you and loves you and likes you. Because of Jesus, you can receive the delight of God as your Father.

Your sin broke your relationship with Him, but the Father wants you back. He sent Jesus to die in your place and cancel your sin. By faith, He then puts His own Spirit in you. He makes His home with you. Now, you are adopted by the Creator of the universe. Now, you can call Him Father. Now, you are home.

WHAT DOES HE WANT TO DO?

What is the primary goal of the Holy Spirit within you? What does He want to do in you? If He's a great teacher, guide, counselor, and helper, then what exactly is His goal?

The bottom line is that the Holy Spirit wants to make you more and more like Jesus. The big, fancy theological word for this is *sanctification*. Sanctification is the transformational process of becoming more like Jesus by partnering with the Holy Spirit within you.

Again, the apostle Paul explains, "And we all, with unveiled face, beholding the glory of the Lord, are being transformed into the same image from one degree of glory to another. For this comes from the Lord who is the Spirit" (2 Corinthians 3:18).

See that "unveiled face" part? Yep, Paul is referencing Moses and the effects of regularly dwelling in the presence of God. When Moses was looking at God face-to-face, his own face began to glow. He was transformed by the presence of God. Paul is saying that in the new covenant, when we behold the glory of Jesus we are transformed into His image from one degree of glory to another. All this is from the Spirit at work within us.

We are transformed day by day, moment by moment, step by step. How? When we regularly fix our attention on Jesus and yield to the Holy Spirit within us, we begin to walk like Him. As we gaze upon Jesus, the Holy Spirit works to fashion and form us into the One we gaze upon. You become like the One you behold. His presence changes you.

Think about it. This is a natural by-product of looking up to someone. You start to talk and act like them. Kobe Bryant's idol was Michael Jordan. He looked up to MJ. He wanted to be like Mike and talk like Mike. He wanted his game to look just like Michael's. So, Kobe studied MJ. He watched him. He spent time with him and learned from him. And guess what? If you listen to Kobe's interviews, you'll see he sounded just like Michael Jordan! His tone of voice and the pace and rate of speech sounded like Mike. And his play on the court was a carbon copy of Michael Jordan.

The same is true for us in the process of sanctification. We look at Jesus and ask the Holy Spirit to form us into His glorious image, from one degree to the next. Over time we will talk like our idol, Jesus. We will think like Him and walk like Him. This is the primary work of the Holy Spirit within you.

FRUIT BEARER—WALK WITH THE SPIRIT

Okay, what does that practically look like on a day-to-day basis? What do we do to partner with the Holy Spirit in this process of sanctification?

The biblical metaphor for this is the image of bearing fruit. Jesus said, "Abide in Me, and you will bear much fruit. Apart from Me you can do nothing" (John 15:4–5, my paraphrase). That word *abide* carries the same connotation as *dwelling*. It means to remain and stay at home with someone—in this case, Jesus. But how do we do that? How do we actively remain with Jesus in our daily lives?

Remember, the Holy Spirit is given to teach us what Jesus taught His disciples. Paul, writing to the Galatian church, uses the metaphor of walking. He explains that this looks like walking by the Spirit and not by the flesh. We can choose to walk according to our own way of thinking or walk submitted to the Holy Spirit within us. He says this "fruit of the Spirit is love, joy, peace, patience, kindness, goodness, faithfulness, gentleness, self-control" (Galatians 5:22–23).

Here's the idea: every experience you have today, either negative or positive, is an opportunity to partner with the Holy Spirit and produce Christlike fruit. This is what the Holy Spirit wants to do within you. This is His agenda for your day—today.

So, when you have a difficult conversation with a family member or coworker later this afternoon, the Holy Spirit is ready to produce Christlike fruit in that conversation. When their words leave you feeling wounded, hurt, and discouraged, this is the time to spend a few moments talking with the Holy Spirit! Here are some questions to ask:

- Holy Spirit, what do you think about what just happened?
- What do you want to do in me that can only be accomplished by walking through this experience together?
- What fruit of Christlikeness needs to come out of me right now?

I've heard preachers and teachers illustrate this point by saying, "When you squeeze an orange tightly, orange juice comes out. When you crush a grape, grape juice comes out. Unfortunately, when some Christians get squeezed by the circumstances of this life, everything *but* Jesus comes out." When you are under pressure and squeezed, does the Holy One come out of your mouth or something far fouler? The call for you and me is to allow the Holy Spirit to form Christlikeness in us in every circumstance of our day.

Try it. The Holy Spirit is with you. Sorry to be so prophetic, but you will encounter a squeezing situation today. When the crush comes, it will be your choice to

1. stay annoyed, frustrated, defeated, and anxious or
2. partner with the Creator of the universe, who dwells within you, to actually form something good out of that experience.

This is totally up to you. It's your choice. Partner with Him or stay frustrated.

Every experience and circumstance in life has a corresponding fruit available to you. Think about where you are right now. What does God want to show you about Himself that is directly related to your situation? He will work all things—good and bad—for your good if you will partner with Him. Here are some examples:

- COVID-19 isolation: God may be teaching you about His peace and rest.
- Coworkers' words: God may be teaching you about His kind-

ness toward you.

- Broken relationship with family or spouse: God may be teaching you about His love.
- Waiting: God may be teaching you about His patience.
- Someone hurts you: God may be teaching you about His healing joy.

Walk through your day, today, aware that everything coming at you, good or bad, is an opportunity to behold the glory of Jesus and bear His fruit in that circumstance. Will you walk by the Spirit today? Will you experience peace today? Again, it's your choice. My prayer is that we will all choose to talk and walk like our idol: Jesus.

Here are some practical steps to take today.

PRACTICAL STEPS

1. Be continually filled with the Holy Spirit. Paul writes, "And do not get drunk with wine, for that is debauchery, but be filled with the Spirit" (Ephesians 5:18). The verb "be filled" in this passage is a command. We are not encouraged to *consider* being filled. No, we are *commanded* to be filled. It's not an "if you get around to it" kind of thing. It's not an "if you are a charismatic believer" kind of thing. No, it's an imperative command in Scripture: be filled with the Holy Spirit.

   That command to be filled is also a passive verb. That means we are commanded to have something done to us. We are not actively filling ourselves with the Spirit. Rather, *someone* is filling us with His Spirit. Our job is to receive.

   Further, the command is not just passive but is present and ongoing. It's a present tense verb that communicates continual action and repetition. We are to be continually filled with the Holy Spirit, and this isn't a one-time shot when we became a Christian—we can and should be continually filled, day by day, maybe even moment by moment.

   To help illustrate this, let us consider one of the biblical metaphors for the Holy Spirit. The Bible speaks of the third member of the Trinity in many ways. For example, Jesus referred to the Holy Spirit as thirst-quenching water that flows from the believer's heart (John 7:37–39). Another biblical metaphor used for the Holy Spirit is wind or breath. This is the imagery of Paul's command. Our hearts are to be like sails that we open to be filled with the wind of the Spirit. We are like boats on the sea who position their heart-sails to be filled with the empowering breath of the Holy Spirit. When we are filled in this way we are propelled to go where the Spirit wants us to go. We are carried along to encounters and moments ordained by God's Spirit within us.

So, practically, what do we do? We ask the Father to fill us with His Spirit, and we receive. Then we can ask again and again. The Spirit is a good gift from our Father in Heaven. Jesus explained, "If you then, who are evil, know how to give good gifts to your children, how much more will the heavenly Father give the Holy Spirit to those who ask him!" (Luke 11:13).

So, when you need help from God, ask to be filled with His Spirit. When you need to be taught something in the Word, ask to be filled with the Spirit and then begin to read the Bible. When you get up in the morning, ask to be filled with the presence of God's Spirit. When you have a business decision to make, ask to be filled with the Spirit and yield to His wisdom. When you pray over your meal at lunch, ask to be filled before you eat. When you lie down to sleep, ask to be filled as you rest. Ask and receive the good gift of the Holy Spirit. This is the command: be continually filled with the Holy Spirit.

2. Live under the loving smile and approval of the Father. A breakthrough moment came for me when I realized that by grace I am considered righteous and approved by the Father every day. What was true of Jesus at His baptism is now true of you and me by faith in Christ.

    We are the Father's beloved kiddos. The Holy Spirit is the love of the Father poured into our hearts to confirm that we are His children. He loves us and is proud of us. He smiles over us all day. He even sings over you in gladness (Zephaniah

3:17).

Before this breakthrough in understanding, I would live my day trying to earn His approval, hoping by the end of the day He would be pleased with me. This meant making sure to get a big quiet time in and not do anything bad. Unfortunately, when I "failed" or didn't achieve 100 percent success, I felt that the Father no longer smiled over me or loved me. I was trying to earn His approval by my good deeds during the day. I felt that His love for me was conditional, based on my behavior.

What changed for me was the realization that when I wake up in the morning, the Father is smiling—and singing—over me. He is delighted in me because I am in Christ and His Spirit dwells within me. This is a much better place to start the day. I am home.

Yes, sometimes I fail and grieve the Spirit in my actions, words, or thoughts. I turn quickly back to the Father. I confess my sin and put my trust in Jesus again. I ask to be filled with the Holy Spirit again, and I receive by faith. Then I continue my day under the Father's smile and delight. That's what it feels like to live at home with the Father, Son, and Holy Spirit. You *can* live your day under His smile and be at home with Him.

Do you ever wonder what the Father is singing when He sings over you during the day? What does the Trinity say when they lovingly discuss your life? Wouldn't it be amazing to hear that conversation and hear God's voice? Well, you can. And that's what we will explore next, in part three of this book.

Part Three

SPEAK, LORD

The boy Samuel ministered before the LORD under Eli. In those days the word of the LORD was rare; there were not many visions. . . . The lamp of God had not yet gone out, and Samuel was lying down in the house of the LORD, where the ark of God was. Then the LORD called Samuel. Samuel answered, "Here I am. . . . Speak, for your servant is listening."

– 1 Samuel 3:1, 3–4, 10 (NIV)

After six days Jesus took Peter, James and John with him and led them up a high mountain, where they were all alone. There he was transfigured before them. His clothes became dazzling white, whiter than anyone in the world could bleach them. And there appeared before them Elijah and Moses, who were talking with Jesus. Peter said to Jesus, "Rabbi, it is good for us to be here. Let us put up three shelters—one for you, one for Moses and one for Elijah." (He did not know what to say, they were so frightened.) Then a cloud appeared and covered them, and a voice came from the cloud: "This is my Son, whom I love. Listen to him!" Suddenly, when they looked around, they no longer saw anyone with them except Jesus.

– Mark 9:2–8 (NIV)

Chapter Seven

READING GOD'S
WORD RELATIONALLY

You search the Scriptures because you think that in them
you have eternal life; and it is they that bear witness about
me, yet you refuse to come to me that you may have life.

– John 5:39–40

My wife and I hang out for fifteen minutes every day without fail.
Here's how it works. Jess has written sixty-six love letters to me over
our marriage. Thirty-nine of those letters she wrote while we were dat-
ing or engaged. She penned the other twenty-seven after we married.

I love her words to me. I've bound them into a large book and read
over the letters every day. I've analyzed the grammar of each sentence.
I've looked up most of the words in a dictionary to understand all the
potential shades of meaning.

Jess stays in a closet in our basement, under the stairs. When I am
ready to read the love letters she wrote, I open the closet door and set a
chair out for her to sit on. I set my timer and then read the love letters
she wrote for me. I've memorized significant portions of her words to
me and am committed to reading through all sixty-six letters over the
course of an entire year.

Her words are so encouraging and make me feel so good about our
marriage. I've highlighted portions of the letters. I've made notes in
the margins. I've had some questions, and I'm still unsure about some
of the things she has written to me. My sense is that if I keep reading

the letters, over time I will understand the parts still unclear to me.

After fifteen minutes, I close the bound letters and put Jess back in the closet under the basement stairs. Having done my duty, I head off about my day.

Our marriage is great.

We are doing great.

I love her so much—especially her letters.

Hopefully you have picked up that this was a pretend scenario. But if it were real, what would you think about my marriage? Would you think that my wife and I are in a good place relationally?

Would you assume we are enjoying the marriage we have? Or would you presume that I was weird, abusive, and disinterested in my wife? You might even think that I cared more for her letters than her.

For years, I'd actually been this way, but not with Jess—I had acted like this with the Father. I have read the Bible cover to cover several times over the last few decades. For some of those years I read the Bible like the scenario above. I read the Bible independent of a relationship with the Author of the Bible. I cared more for the Word than the Father. Sadly, I didn't love Him. I loved His Word.

Here's what you need to understand in this chapter. The Bible is not the goal or the prize. The Bible is a means toward getting the prize. The goal of Bible reading is relational intimacy with the Father who loves you. *He* is the prize.

The Father breathed out these sixty-six books to reveal Himself and to draw you into a relationship with Him. The great danger, though, is when we think that reading the Bible for fifteen minutes while ignoring Him the rest of the day is okay.

The spiritual discipline of Bible reading is significant and formative for every believer. We should be in the Word, yes. But we should read the Word *relationally*. The goal of Bible reading is relational transformation, not academic information. The prize of Bible reading is not learning that friendship with God is theologically possible. Rather, the prize of Bible reading is experiencing a growing friendship with God.

WHAT IS THE BIBLE?

The Bible contains the words of a loving Father, written for His children. They tell His kids what He's like and how He thinks and acts. He has recorded these words to communicate to us. This communication is not a textbook but rather a love story about how we have run away from Him and the lengths to which He has gone to get us back to Himself.

The Protestant Bible contains sixty-six books, divided into two large sections: before Christ and after Christ. The Old Testament contains thirty-nine books written before Christ, while the New Testament contains twenty-seven books written after Christ. The Father chose to pen these words through over thirty human authors, over some fifteen hundred years, in Hebrew, Greek, and Aramaic. These books include multiple literary genres including history, law, songs, poetry, biographies, letters, and prophecies. All these words communicate the truth: God saying, "I want to be with you."

It is imperative for you to understand that the Bible is not a book of rules you must obey to be loved by an angry, upset God. Rather, this is a book that invites you into a relationship with a Father who loves you.

I grew up a Southern Baptist and thank God for this. I was raised to love the Bible. I'm a "Word" guy in the deepest part of my soul. Daily Bible reading has been the single most important discipline of my entire life. No other practice has had a more transformative impact on my life than Bible reading.

But when I learned the truth of this chapter, my Bible reading changed forever. For years, my discipline was to read and memorize Scripture every day. That was good. It was not a waste of time because the Holy Spirit used all those years of consuming the Word to shape me. Yet I spent many years reading the text academically and not relationally. And I'm not the first one to do this.

YOU SEARCH THE SCRIPTURES

Jesus once had a conversation with some biblical scholars. They were well-read in and well-respected teachers of the Scriptures. They knew the original languages. They knew the critical arguments. They had devoted themselves to daily reading of the Scriptures. These guys knew their Bible inside and out.

There was only one problem. They missed the entire point of the Scriptures. When the Author of the words they had memorized and devoted their lives to was standing in front of them, they missed Him. In fact, they went on to kill Him.

This is a sobering encounter. For a "Bible" guy like me, this conversation makes me shudder. These "Bible" guys believed that reading the Bible daily, memorizing it, and understanding it thoroughly would give them life. Yet Jesus said to them, "You search the Scriptures because you think that in them you have eternal life; and it is they that bear witness about me, yet you refuse to come to me that you may have life" (John 5:39–40). They failed to realize that life was found in the Author of the Word, not in the words themselves. They were so deluded they couldn't even see the point of the Scriptures when He stood right in front of them!

How often have I done the same thing? I read my Bible passage for the day and feel accomplished but never engage at a relational level with Jesus while I'm reading. I set my timer and read His words at Him but never personally engage with Him.

That is the first delusion: missing out on friendship with Jesus by not reading the Bible relationally. The second delusion is equally dangerous: reading the Bible with no intention to put into practice the commands of a Father who loves you.

IMPORTANCE OF RELATIONAL OBEDIENCE

Jesus' half-brother James warned others about this delusional form of Bible reading. He said, "Be doers of the word, and not hearers only, deceiving yourselves" (James 1:22). In other words, "Do not deceive yourself by listening to God's Word without practicing it." It is possible to read the Bible and waste your time.

What's worse is that you will be deceived into thinking that this is normal. Let me be clear: it is not normal to read the commands of a Father who loves you and not obey Him. This lack of obedience demonstrates that we are not reading the Bible relationally. We condition ourselves to believe that it is okay to hear the Word, listen to the Word, and study the Word, but not actively respond in obedience. Without intentional practice of what you are learning, you are deceiving yourself and ignoring the Father who loves you.

Let me illustrate it this way. One day I leave to go to work. I want Caden, my son, to do two things before I get back. One, clean up his room; and two, feed Bear, the dog. I write a note and leave it on the kitchen table:

> Hey Bubba, I love you and I am so proud of you! I'm praying that you have a great day today. Please clean your room and feed Bear.
>
> Thanks, Pops

After a full day of work, I return home and see the note is gone. I head over to Caden's room and hear voices. Curious, I open his bedroom door and see a gathering of kids sitting in a circle with Caden. Each kid has a copy of my letter in their hands. Some of the copies have highlighted portions, underlining, and notes written on the sides of my text.

I ask Caden what's going on, and he informs me that he was so encouraged by my note that he called all his friends to join him in reading it together. He tells me that one of the older kids in the group is really good at grammar and talking. So they collected some piggy-bank money and asked the "grammar kid" to go through my note word for word and explain all the shades of meaning I was intending to communicate in the message. They have committed to memorizing every word. Also, the plan is to spend individual time at home, looking up all the words in a dictionary, and being prepared to discuss with the group next week.

Confused, I pull Caden aside and ask him if he cleaned his room and fed the dog. He said he forgot and ran out of time because he was too busy organizing this group to study the note I left him.

RELATIONALLY MOTIVATED OBEDIENCE

It is a ridiculous example, isn't it? But don't we do the same thing with God and His Word? I have. I have been deceived and I have deceived myself. I've read the Bible and not put into practice what I've read. I have conditioned myself to think that this is normal. But it's not normal to read the words of a friend who loves you and then completely ignore them.

Reading the Bible relationally means being willing to be confronted with things that need to change in your life as the Father shows them to you. Again, this is one of the goals of the Holy Spirit in your life. He is ready to partner with you and help you obey the Father's words. This partnering work of obedience will form you more and more into the image of Jesus.

One last thing to mention about obedience. Did you notice how I started my letter to Caden? I communicated at least three things before asking him to obey my request. First, I called him by an intimate name—Bubba. This is how I lovingly refer to Caden. He is my boy. He is my bubba. You have been created and called by name too. The Father chose you, called you by name, and loves you. He desires intimacy and friendship with you because He is a good Father.

Second, I affirmed my love for him and communicated that I am proud of him *before* I asked him to do something for me. Notice the important distinction here. I love Caden and am proud of him because he is my son, *not* because he obeys me. The letter does not communicate that my love for him is conditional or tied to his obedience.

Many followers of Jesus obey the Bible in an attempt to earn the Father's love. This is not the gospel. The order is significant: because we are loved, then we *get* to respond to that gracious relationship with glad obedience. We obey Him because we have experienced amazing grace and love.

Finally, notice that I express my care for the rest of his day and not just what I have asked him to do for me. I care about Caden as a person and the man he is becoming. This analogy breaks down because God is with us all the time; however, notice that a good father is more interested in who you are becoming *with* him rather than what you do *for* him.

This is an important concept to nail down. Obedience is relational. Obedience is motivated by indestructible love. Obedience is more about who you are becoming rather than what you are doing. Stay relationally connected to the Father, Son, and Holy Spirit. This relationship will transform your Bible reading.

PRACTICAL STEPS

1. Get the Word in you. I cannot stress this enough. Whatever you do, consume the Bible. It is spiritual food, and without it you will starve. I can actually feel my spirit drying up and shriveling when I'm not reading and consuming the Scriptures.

    Find a translation you will read, and start reading every day. If you find that difficult, get an audio version of that translation and listen to the Word. Whatever you do, get the Word in you. As you read and listen, you will learn God's vocabulary and the way He thinks. Get the Word in you.

2. Stay relationally connected to Jesus as you read. This is not a normal book. You don't read the Bible the way you read a newspaper or a novel. Because of the indwelling Holy Spirit—God Himself—you have the author with you! Jesus is sitting right next to you while you read, so acknowledge Him. Don't be like the scholars who missed Him standing right in front of them.

    After you read a sentence or two, stop and ask the Holy Spirit to speak to you about the text. Imagine Jesus pointing out the words of the text and explaining them to you. Seriously. Read the Bible under the smile of the Father. Read relationally, in His presence.

3. Do not settle for academic information, but expect relational transformation as you read. When you approach the Bible, don't think of it as a dry and clinical textbook. Consider it as highly flammable words that the Holy Spirit intends to ignite and pour over your heart.

    After His resurrection, Jesus was walking with two of His disciples who did not realize it was Him. He was teaching them as they walked to a town called Emmaus. After this encounter, they said to each other, "Did not our hearts burn within us while he talked to us on the road, while he opened to us the Scriptures?" (Luke 24:32).

The Bible is not "safe," especially when you read it relationally. Read and expect fire to come into your life. Yes, sometimes I read the Bible and it's boring. In those moments, I ask Jesus to burn His truth within me. I ask for His fire to blaze in my heart as I read.

4.   Partner with the Holy Spirit to be a "doer" of the Word. This is closely tied to the previous practical point. When we read the Scriptures and don't obey what we are reading, we delude ourselves. What transforms us is acting on what we learn from the Holy Spirit as we read.

Like I said, the Bible is not safe. The Holy Spirit is not safe. The goal is transformation and change. When you read the Bible, expect the process to change you and for the Holy Spirit to form you more into the image of Jesus every day. Don't read casually. Read with intention and purpose. Read for transformation and not just information.

For example, when you read a passage, ask the Holy Spirit to teach you. Picture Jesus with you, stop, and listen. Ask the Father, "What are You saying to me in this passage, and what do You want me to do today in response to what You've shown me?"

If you read the Bible in the morning, the next twenty-four hours should look different based on what you read and what you heard. This is called application. It could be showing love to your neighbor by mowing their side of the lawn that bumps up to yours. It could be a call to your kids to ask for their forgiveness because the Holy Spirit revealed that you sinned against them with your harsh words the day before. It could be a challenge to share about your faith in Jesus with a coworker during the lunch break.

Don't just read the Bible. Be prepared to have the Holy Spirit change you and call you to act on what you are learning.

5.   Finally, share what you learned that day from your relational reading of the Bible with one other person. If you read in the morning, there will be an opportunity during the day to share

what you've learned. I have had some of the most amazing encounters when I share what I have learned with someone I meet during the day.

Embrace this adventure. The Holy Spirit wants to teach you and then speak through you to someone else. Everything I'm writing in this book has come from revelation that the Father has given to me over years of reading relationally with Him, and I'm delighted to now share it with you.

You can receive this kind of revelation too. You can hear the voice of Jesus speak directly to your circumstances during the day—even without the Bible in your hand. How? That's what we will consider in the next chapter: how to hear God's voice.

Chapter Eight

PRAYER AND HEARING GOD'S VOICE

My sheep hear my voice, and I know them,
and they follow me.

– John 10:27

The most referenced animal in the Bible, by far, is the sheep. This fluffy creature is mentioned more often than the lion, serpent, dove, donkey, and even leviathan. Why? Because one of the primary metaphors used to describe the relationship between God and His people is the shepherd and his sheep. It is a persistent and pervasive metaphor.

DAILY LIFE-RHYTHM WITH THE SHEPHERD—PSALM 23

The Old Testament passage that most perfectly describes this relationship is Psalm 23. David, the shepherd-king, penned this psalm of comfort, presence, and dependence. David, a human shepherd, reflects on his relationship with God, the Divine Shepherd. Psalm 23 pictures the daily life of a shepherd and his sheep. As day breaks, the shepherd leads the sheep to graze and water. After they have eaten, the shepherd leads the sheep to rest. At the end of the day, the shepherd leads the sheep home, protects them from predators, and cares for their wounds.

One of the most significant theological truths from Psalm 23 is that sheep are dependent on their shepherd every day of their lives. They don't worry about which pasture they will graze in, nor do they concern themselves about which path to take to the stream. They trust the shepherd and follow him day after day. The daily lives of the sheep are centered around the shepherd and where he leads them.

How about you? Is your everyday rhythm oriented more toward God or your daily planner? Do you find yourself anxious about what is coming up on your schedule, or do you trust that the Shepherd will provide and protect you over the next twenty-four hours?

You may think that this orientation is over the top. Surely, one cannot expect to live their life like this. We have things to do, businesses to run, people to lead, and problems to solve. We don't have time to sit around and graze all day.

What motivates my thoughts on this is not a desire to sit around and graze but to orient my daily life around the Shepherd. David was Israel's greatest human king, and he understood the value of a life centered on God. He had a kingdom to run, an entire nation to lead, and enemies on all sides. Yet David understood that dependence on the Shepherd is priority whether one is resting or working.

We were created to enjoy a daily rhythm of life with the Shepherd. This is much different than a typical fifteen minute "quiet time" to start the day. No, this is a twenty-four-hour rhythm of life with the Father. All day. Every day.

I AM THE GOOD SHEPHERD

Jesus picks up the Old Testament theme of sheep and shepherd and explicitly declares Himself to be God. He says, "The thief comes only to steal and kill and destroy. I came that they may have life and have it abundantly. I am the good shepherd. The good shepherd lays down his life for the sheep" (John 10:10–11).

Jesus is saying that He is God, the Good Shepherd, who cares for His sheep. He is the Shepherd who provides, protects, and guides His sheep. He explains that the danger is real. We have an enemy, and his goal, like in the garden, is to steal, kill, and destroy us. But there is a Shepherd who has come to save us from the enemy's plan. Jesus has come to give us abundant life.

How? He has willingly laid down His life for us. We are the lost sheep who have wandered far away from God, and Jesus the Good

Shepherd died on the cross to rescue us and bring us back into His fold. The prophet Isaiah spoke of this Messiah-Shepherd: "But he was pierced for our transgressions; he was crushed for our iniquities; upon him was the chastisement that brought us peace, and with his wounds we are healed. All we like sheep have gone astray; we have turned—every one—to his own way; and the LORD has laid on him the iniquity of us all" (Isaiah 53:5–6).

On the cross, Jesus took your sin, in your place. You and I deserved to die because of our wandering feet and rebellious hearts. Jesus left His throne to come and rescue you—a wayward sheep—because He loves you. He was crucified and then raised from the dead to triumph over the enemy, over your sin, and over death itself.

Here's a picture of a shepherd laying down his life for his sheep. On July 9, 2020, a six-year-old boy named Bridger Walker was walking with his sister in their hometown of Cheyenne, Wyoming. Bridger noticed a ferocious dog charging his sister with the intention of causing her harm. Without worrying about his own safety, he stepped between the dog and his sister. He took on the attack so that his sister would be safe. Bridger was bitten several times on the face and head but managed to grab his sister's hand and run with her to safety. Interviewed after the event, Bridger said, "If someone had to die, I thought it should be me."[3]

My friend, this is love. We are loved by the Creator of the universe. We had wandered. We had rejected Him. We were headed for death because of our sin and rebellion. Jesus, though innocent and righteous, came to die in our place. By His death and resurrection, we can be free of sin, brokenness, the enemy, and death.

This is good news. This is the gospel. Nothing can separate us from His love. We are loved by a God who wants to shepherd us all day, every day. He wants to be with us. He wants to talk with us and grow in friendship with us.

PRAYER AS RELATIONAL CONVERSATION

Jesus didn't die on the cross to save you and then leave you to flail along through life alone. The Father didn't send His Spirit to dwell within you and then expect you to figure out life all by yourself, clueless. No, He wants to be with you and guide you *today*. He wants to walk with you and talk with you *today*.

This is what prayer is all about. Prayer is conversation with the Shepherd, as a friend, all day.

For a long time, I saw prayer as a discipline that I had to engage in to be a good Christian kid. Again, I would set my timer and then talk at God for the prescribed time. Usually this was me asking Him for things that I wanted (or thought I wanted).

By the way, that's not a bad thing. We should approach the throne of grace with confidence and make our requests to the Father. However, prayer is much more than asking God for things. Prayer is conversation. Prayer is a relational activity of talking with, and listening to, the Good Shepherd.

Jesus said, "My sheep hear my voice, and I know them, and they follow me" (John 10:27). Even today, shepherds in the Middle East can call out into a mixed group of mingled sheep and divide the flocks simply by calling them. Shepherds are constant companions to their sheep. The sheep know their shepherd's voice and presence. They understand his authority and leadership in their lives. When he calls, they follow.

When I began to understand prayer as a daily rhythm of conversation with the Shepherd as a friend, my prayer life was transformed. I wasn't content with a timer set for fifteen minutes because I realized I could talk to Him all day. And He wants to talk back to me. He wants to guide my plans, my day, my conversations, my goals—everything. He is a Good Shepherd.

We will never grow in deep friendship with Jesus if we are always talking *at* Him and never listening *to* Him. Have you ever been around a person who never listens to you because they are always talking? They never stop to listen and understand what you think about a situation. My guess is that you are probably not very close to that person, right? It is the same with Jesus. Prayer can become very one-sided if we are always talking and never listening. This imbalanced prayer does not create friendship with Him. That's like having a sheep that is always "baaing" at the shepherd and never listening.

For me, that's why prayer was so hard. I was doing it wrong. I kept talking and never listening. But then I discovered that if I just stop and listen, the Shepherd has *a lot* to say to me during my day. Seriously.

This has changed my life and transformed my relationship with Jesus. This is how you "pray without ceasing" (1 Thessalonians 5:17) because you can be talking and listening all day. Prayer doesn't have to be fifteen minutes in the morning and forty seconds before each meal. Now, that's good. Keep doing that. But then consider talking and listening all day. Pray without ceasing. Prayer is designed to be a daily life-rhythm with the Shepherd.

Below are ten practical steps in conversational prayer and hearing the voice of the Good Shepherd.

TEN PRACTICAL STEPS TO HEARING THE SHEPHERD'S VOICE

1. Know that He wants to speak to you, and thank Him. Spend a few moments of gratefulness, because the Good Shepherd loves you and wants to engage with you today. Thank Jesus for dying for you and bringing you freedom. Thank Him for the blessings you get to enjoy with Him today. Begin with thanksgiving.

2. Read the Bible to learn Jesus' vocabulary and speech patterns. This is the fastest way to hear Jesus' voice. Those are His words. The Bible is what Jesus sounds like. Time spent reading the Bible develops your ear to recognize Jesus' vocabulary and communication style. If you want to know what Jesus sounds like and the words He uses, get the Word in you.

3. Be still, and picture Jesus with you. The excessive noise around many of us drowns out the Shepherd's voice. When you are first growing in this practice, it may be helpful to get away to a quiet place and be still. Close your eyes, take a couple of deep breaths, and fix your eyes on Jesus. Picture Jesus standing or sitting next to you. Your imagination is a gift from the Father, so use it to engage with Him.

4. Ask Him a question. Whatever is on your mind, ask Him. You may ask Jesus something like "Jesus, what do you think about me?" or "Jesus, what is on Your heart and mind for me right now?" You could also ask Him, "Jesus, what would you like to say to me?" If you are reading a

Bible passage, you could ask Him a question about that Scripture.

5. Watch and listen. This is key. Don't skip this. If you want to grow in friendship and intimacy with Jesus, you must stop talking and start listening. I say this lovingly: stop talking when you pray. At first you may be anxious, thinking you won't see or hear anything. Relax. He is a Good Shepherd who wants to talk to you. Look at Jesus and wait. Take the same position as Mary, who sat at her Rabbi's feet and listened to Him speak (Luke 10:38–42).

6. Write down what you see, hear, or experience. Whatever happens, write it down. I use a computer for my journaling, so I can close my eyes and type what I see, hear, or experience. Whatever impression you have, even if it seems like it came from your own thoughts, write it down. Do not analyze it. Simply write it down. This is so you can be present with Jesus and get the information down on paper or screen. Then, afterward you will test what you wrote down. But not right now. Write down everything you see, hear, or experience.

7. Rest in His presence. Remember the good news that you don't have to prove yourself. Take advantage of this silence with Jesus. You don't have to talk. He doesn't have to talk. Again, this may take some practice, but it is worth it. You know you are growing in friendship with someone when you can sit together in silence and just be together. Remind yourself of the gospel: you don't have to prove yourself to Jesus. You don't have to do anything for Him. He wants to be with you. Sheep aren't stressed about what the Shepherd thinks of them. He leads them beside still waters and restores their soul. Rest in this truth and in His presence. You might even experience physical, spiritual, and emotional healing just resting in His presence.

8. Test what you saw and heard according to Scripture and with your community. We do need to be wise about what we see, hear, or experience. Just because you hear something doesn't necessarily mean that it was from Jesus. It might be your own thoughts or what you've heard from

others or the world. So you need to compare what you've written with Scripture. Jesus' voice will never contradict His written words, so you can compare and test to see if what you heard is from Him or not. You can also examine the fruit that is produced in your heart by what you wrote. If the words bring hope, joy, peace, and a sense of being deeply loved, then they are probably from Jesus. If not, then simply ignore them. Also, submit what you've written to the church community in your life. Let someone else read what you believe you have heard, and ask them for their input. Test what you are hearing by Scripture and community.

9. Walk through your day with Jesus near you, and keep listening. Regularly, throughout the day, picture Jesus with you and ask Him what He thinks about what you are doing in the moment. As I mentioned earlier, I have an alarm that goes off every hour on my phone. This reminds me to stay present with the Shepherd and look up from what I'm doing to see where He is and what He thinks about what I'm doing. Keep asking Him questions. Keep listening. Before you walk into a staff meeting at work, ask Jesus what He thinks about the plans you are going to discuss. Listen. Before you go to sleep at night, ask Jesus what He thought about your day together. Confess the times where you missed Him, and thank Him for the times you were in sync and present with Him.

10. Finally, ask the Father for greater sensitivity to His voice. He is happy to answer this request. Ask that He would give you more of the Holy Spirit, who is the Spirit of wisdom and revelation. Ask that the eyes and ears of your heart would be opened to the hope and glory of Jesus (Ephesians 1:15–22). Ask for more, and expect greater sensitivity to the voice of the Good Shepherd.

The previous two chapters have been setting the stage for the last chapter in this section. We will explore what happens to you as you read the Bible relationally and grow to hear the Shepherd's voice during the day. In the next chapter, we'll learn how the voice of God shapes us.

Chapter Nine

HIS VOICE SHAPES YOU

You are my beloved Son; with you I am well pleased.

– Luke 3:22

Fear not, for I have redeemed you; I have called you by name, you are mine. . . . You are precious in my eyes, and honored, and I love you.

– Isaiah 43:1,4

The primary fig leaf that I've fashioned and clothed myself with during my life is approval. From as early as I can remember, I've cared too much what others think of me. This has driven much of the narrative of my life. *What will they think if I do this? How disappointed will they be if I say no? What if they don't like me?* This voice has been a persistent companion throughout my life and has shaped me.

Every voice you consistently listen to and agree with will shape your identity. You become who you listen to the most. You are transformed by the voice you accept. Carefully consider what voice you are listening to and how it is transforming you.

ENGLAND

When I was in eighth grade, my family moved to Nottingham, England, for a year. My dad took a sabbatical leave for study, and the entire Moore clan went with him. That year was a foundational year for me. It was amazing, and it was painful.

My birthday is in June, and I'd never gotten to celebrate with my classmates because the American school system takes summers off. In England, however, schools are year-round, and I was excited to finally celebrate my birthday with classmates and friends.

The school day itself was uneventful. I went to classes, and my friends wished me a happy birthday. It was great. Then after the bell rang, while I was walking to the bus to ride home and celebrate with my family, it happened. A kid ran up behind me and yelled, "Happy birthday!" and smashed his hand onto my head. It was surprising and shocking, especially since I knew him—and we were not friends. He was a bully. He hated me because I was an American.

Another one of his friends ran past and hit me over the head too. At this point I noticed something in my hair. Rubbing my head and then examining my hand, I saw sticky yolk and white shell. Two eggs had been smashed on my head.

Time stood still. Everything slowed down. Even my thinking felt sluggish. I didn't have time to think about why I had egg on my head when two handfuls of flour came crashing down over me. Then a healthy glug of oil. A crowd gathered and began pelting me with eggs.

Laughter. Mocking. Pointing. Crushed eggs and a crushed heart.

The bus pulled up, the crowd left, and I stood stunned. What should I do? I couldn't get on the bus like this. My Harry Potter look-a-like school uniform was a sticky mess. So, I walked back into the school and called my dad on the other side of town. The principal assured me this is normal behavior for one's birthday.

By the way, I looked it up, and it's true that sometimes friends will "egg" someone on their birthday. The difference was that the ringleader of this egging was not my friend, and his goal was to humiliate me.

I walked to the gym shower room, put my backpack down on the tile floor, started the shower, and sat down fully clothed under the water. I wept. This was not how I expected my first school birthday to go down. I felt rejected and alone.

My dad showed up and hugged me. We drove home. He was furious—and rightfully so. He made some calls and did what any good father would do. As a father now, I can imagine the anger he experienced. For the rest of my birthday, I sat in stunned silence, trying to process what had just happened.

TRANSFORMING VOICES

Everyone has painful experiences. They mark us. For me, I began to believe the voice that said I wasn't worth loving or being friends with. I would agree with the voice that said, "You have to be perfect, funny, smart, likeable, and athletic, and then maybe they will like you—but probably not." This voice stoked the fear of never being known or loved.

Listening to this voice and accepting it shaped my identity. It shaped the way I saw myself. It lied to me, and my response was to make fig leaves called "approval" and "other people's opinion" to cover my pain, shame, and hurt.

My identity became an imposter that would say and do things to keep everyone liking me. This pretender craved the approval of friends, family, and those around me. Keeping it fed was exhausting work.

That is the problem with fig leaves. They don't really solve the shame problem. We saw that in chapter 1. Deep down, I knew I wasn't really being "me." I was exhausted being someone I thought would be liked by everyone around me. I had to prove that I was worthy of love. And when I was "accepted," the voice would whisper accusingly, "Yeah, but they love your imposter, not the real you. If they knew the real Jamie, they wouldn't like you anymore."

To shut down that terrifying thought, I just fed the imposter more and more. I worked harder. Lied better. Smiled more. This left me emotionally exhausted, trying to prove myself in every interaction. Over and over again. I was around people but felt alone. I was loved by family and friends but couldn't receive it fully. I was afraid, and I was alone.

RECEIVING IDENTITY

After that year, we moved back to Texas as a family. I started high school and joined the marching band and choir program. All the girls loved my British accent. Unfortunately, it faded by Christmas. What didn't fade, though, was the fig leaf of image and approval. I wasn't "me" to anyone. I was still trying to be funny, smart, likeable, and someone worth loving.

We started attending University Baptist Church, across the street from the Texas Christian University campus. I joined the youth choir and began to build a new life with new friends at church. One of the greatest gifts the Father has ever given me is singing in that youth choir. We led worship every Sunday morning in the first service and sang a choral anthem each week from memory. The words of those songs were all Scripture based, and I was memorizing them and singing them every week. The words of Jesus were being planted deep in my heart. What I can see now, nearly thirty years later, is that those words would be used to counter the lying voice I had been hearing. The Father, Son, and Holy Spirit were planting Scripture deep into my heart, and those words would grow into a massive oak of identity in the years to come.

I thank God for planting His Words deep inside of me. One song I remember to this day was written by Craig Courtney entitled, "Be Not Afraid." The text is taken from Isaiah 43, and I still weep when I hear it sung. The text is God, speaking to His people.

> Be not afraid
> For I have redeemed you
> Be not afraid
> I have called you by name
> When you pass through the waters
> I will be with you
> When you pass through the floods
> They will not sweep o'er you
> When you walk through the fire
> You will not be consumed
> You are mine
> You are precious in my sight
> My love for you is everlasting
> My love for you shall have no end
> When you pass through the waters

I will be with you
When you pass through the floods
They will not sweep o'er you
When you walk through the fire
You will not be consumed
You are mine
You are precious in my sight[4]

I encourage you to go to my YouTube channel to watch the actual recording of my youth choir singing this song thirty-some years ago![5]

The Father planted His words deep in my heart: You are mine. You are precious in my sight. For decades, these words and others like them have been growing silently and imperceptibly inside me. Like a small mustard seed, the words of the Father have grown into a massive shade tree of identity. I may feel alone, but the truth is that my Father in heaven will be with me in every circumstance of my life.

I may feel rejected, but the truth is that I was chosen, redeemed, and rescued by my Creator and Savior Jesus Christ.

I may feel unloved, but the truth is that the love of the Father and the Son has been poured into my heart by the Holy Spirit. God will never leave me nor abandon me. Nothing can separate me from the love of the Father, in Christ, sealed by the Holy Spirit. Nothing.

How is this possible? My primary identity is not my family of origin or job or my degrees or my accomplishments or what anyone thinks of me. Each of those secondary identity markers is susceptible to loss. I could lose my job, my family, my accomplishments, or my reputation at any time, but I can't lose my primary identity in Jesus. It is given to me by the Father in heaven. He tells me who I am. He says, "You are mine. You are precious in My sight."

I have placed my faith in Jesus' sacrificial death and resurrection for my sin and brokenness. Jesus and I have traded identities: He became my sin and died on the cross in my place, while I received His righteousness and perfection. Jesus took my identity and gave me His. He took my fig leaves of shame and guilt and fear, and the Father has clothed me in Jesus' righteousness (2 Corinthians 5:21). I don't have to prove myself to God or to anyone else.

When the Father looks at me, because I am in Christ He sees His child. Because of Jesus, I can receive the words of the Father, and so can you. You can hear Him say, "Do not fear, for I have redeemed you; I have summoned you by name; you are mine. . . . I will be with you. . . . You are precious and honored in my sight. . . . I love you" (Isaiah 43:1–4, my paraphrase).

You see, perfect love casts out fear (1 John 4:18). What I was most afraid of was being rejected, unloved, and alone. That is impossible because of Jesus.

PROCESS OF SHAPING IDENTITY

Did I sing this song in high school, and everything changed in an instant? No. I wish that were true. The truth is it has been a process of being shaped and molded by Jesus' words rather than another voice in my head.

It hasn't been a straight line from "alone and afraid" to "loved and approved," either. There have been ups and downs. There have been seasons when I lived my life in full assurance of my identity in Christ. I was open to others and felt free to be in Christ before others.

Then there would be times when the voice of fear and approval would speak again. I would forget that I am loved fully by the Father. I would slip back into trying to prove myself as lovable to others and even God Himself. I even began to use spiritual disciplines as fig leaves of approval. The disciplined Christian walk became a way of earning God's love. If I missed reading the Bible one morning, I felt bad and unlovable. If I did read the Bible, then I felt that He loved me. The enemy played me; his voice encouraged me to use spiritual disciplines as fig leaves. This is a deadly trick, my friend.

If you listen to this voice, you will believe that the Father's love is dependent on your obedience to Him. You will believe that if you give money, pray, read the Bible, serve others, go to church and all the other "Christian" stuff, *then* the Father will love you. You will come to think that doing something can earn His love.

The gospel truth is that nothing you do will get the Father to love you more than He does in Jesus. He loves you with an everlasting, eternal, inexhaustible love that is freely given to you by faith in Christ!

You cannot do anything to get a single ounce more of His love. He gave His love freely and infinitely.

Breakthrough came when I realized this truth. Now, obeying the Father was something I wanted to do because I was already eternally loved. Obeying the Father from this place of secure identity in His love is the way He has designed us to function as Christians. That is the voice of Jesus. Then you can love and be present with others. You don't need to be fake or try to manipulate someone's opinion of you, because you are securely loved by your Father in heaven.

This is true freedom, friend—free to love those around you with no strings attached because you are securely loved and approved by the Creator of the universe.

So, how do we practically experience the Father's loving voice in a way that shapes us? Here are some practical steps to take today.

PRACTICAL STEPS

1. Not to sound like a broken record, but get the Word inside you by any means available. Do it. I wouldn't be where I am today if I hadn't had the words of Isaiah 43 implanted deep in my fragile ninth-grade heart. Also, the breakthrough would have come much slower if I hadn't read the Bible daily for years. You will learn who you are in Christ most surely by reading the Bible. Over time, the Holy Spirit will shape your identity as you read and consume the Word.

2. Start a list of identity statements from the Bible. Go on a treasure hunt to find out who the Father says you are in Christ. Begin with the letters of Paul. Usually the first half of his individual letters teach about our identity in Christ. A great first chapter to start with is Romans 8. Read it every day for a week, and write out all the identity statements you find. I'll get you started. The first identity statement of Romans 8 is this: you are no longer condemned if you are in Christ Jesus (that's verse 1). After you've finished reading Romans 8, go to Ephesians, then Philippians, then come back and read all of Romans. Jump over to 1 Peter and 1 John, then read the entire New Testament. Keep writing down all the identity

statements. When you hear the voice of fear, go back and read those statements from Scripture, and remind yourself of who you are in Christ!

3. When you mess up and sin, remind yourself of the gospel. Remember the good news, confess your sin, and run back into the arms of the Father. Don't wait for the voice of accusation to say, "You messed up. He won't take you back this time. It's too late." Tell that voice to go to literal hell, and then run back into the arms of the Father. Receive forgiveness. You *will* mess up. When you do, don't wait. Go to the Father by faith in Jesus. Restored identity is found in the Father. I've created a personal list of "Gospel Scriptures" that I have memorized and use regularly. If you would like a free copy, check it out here: https://www.jamiemoore.org/friendshipfreebies.

4. Check your motivation when you begin to do something "for" God. Before going to church or engaging in a ministry activity, take a quick heart check to see what is motivating your behavior. Ask Jesus, "Am I doing this to earn Your love and approval, or am I doing this because I am eternally loved already?" Trust me, serving from a place of identity is much better and easier than serving to prove yourself.

5. Finally, check your motivations before and during social interactions with others. Before I walk into a meeting, I stop and check my heart to see if I'm secure in Christ or if I'm feeling insecure. I check to see if my heart is resting in the gospel or if I am trying to prove myself to the people I'm meeting with. Ask yourself, "Where am I? Do I have any fig leaves on right now?" While you are in conversation, check your heart as well. Check to see if you are speaking in a way to impress the other person or to get them to like you. Ask, "Am I trying to prove myself right now?"

The voice of the Good Shepherd brings life, peace, identity, security, and joy. Growing in friendship with God means intentionally seeking His words and His voice, which shape you over time.

So far in this book we have explored the first two components of friendship with God: seeking His face and seeking His voice. In this last section, we will look at the final ingredient: seeking His hands and feet by joining Him on His mission in the world.

Part Four

SEND ME!

In the year that King Uzziah died I saw the Lord sitting upon a throne, high and lifted up; and the train of his robe filled the temple. Above him stood the seraphim. Each had six wings: with two he covered his face, and with two he covered his feet, and with two he flew. And one called to another and said:

"Holy, holy, holy is the Lord of hosts;
the whole earth is full of his glory!"

And the foundations of the thresholds shook at the voice of him who called, and the house was filled with smoke. And I said: "Woe is me! For I am lost; for I am a man of unclean lips, and I dwell in the midst of a people of unclean lips; for my eyes have seen the King, the Lord of hosts!"

Then one of the seraphim flew to me, having in his hand a burning coal that he had taken with tongs from the altar. And he touched my mouth and said: "Behold, this has touched your lips; your guilt is taken away, and your sin atoned for."

And I heard the voice of the Lord saying, "Whom shall I send, and who will go for us?" Then I said, "Here I am! Send me."

– Isaiah 6:1–8

Chapter Ten

COMMISSIONED IN HIS PRESENCE

As the Father has sent me, even so I am sending you.
– John 20:21

The Father has another goal, beyond being with you and talking with you. He also wants to work powerfully through you.

The goal of your life is not only to enjoy Him but to help others enjoy relationship with the Father too. He is shaping you by His voice and Word, not just for your good but for the good of others. The Father desires to bless you, and then He intends to bless others through you. This is the pattern found throughout Scripture called *commissioning*.

Abraham, Gideon, Isaiah, and Jesus' disciples are all examples of this commissioning. Each encountered God, heard Him speak, received revelation and identity, and were sent out to bless those around them. Let's look at each of these commissioning encounters.

ABRAHAM: BLESSED TO BLESS OTHERS

Genesis 12 introduces an important character. The Tower of Babel incident had just occurred. The nations were scattered, and the languages confused. In one of these nations, a man named Abram was minding his own business when God appeared to him.

This was God's choice and initiative. He encountered Abram and promised to bless him and be with him. He called Abram to follow Him, step by step, to a new land. God would be with Abram every step of the way. Even though Abram and his wife, Sarai, were childless and well past child-bearing years, God promised to give them children and bless them. God changed Abram's name to Abraham, which means "father of nations." (Sarai's name, too, was changed, to Sarah.)

Abraham and Sarah encountered God, heard His voice, and received new identities. Their new identities were given for the purpose of blessing all the nations of the world. The problem was that they didn't have any children, and Abraham, at one hundred years old, and Sarah, at ninety, would need a miracle to conceive.

That's exactly what God did. He chose them. He called them. He changed their names. And then He gave them a son, Isaac. Isaac would have a son named Jacob. This Jacob would have his own encounter with God and a name change as well. Jacob wrestled with God and became Israel. Through the people of Israel, the Messianic King would come and bless all the peoples of the earth. This king is Jesus Christ.

So, here's the commissioning pattern. Abram encounters God. Abram receives a new and unique identity in God's presence. He and Sarah were barren before encountering God. Now they will be fruitful and multiply because God is with them. Abraham walks with God and follows Him. God blesses entire generations of people through Abraham.

God's presence and voice changed Abraham into a fruitful father and made him a blessing to nations.

GIDEON: MIGHTY MAN OF VALOR

Judges 6 introduces another important character named Gideon. The people of Israel had been experiencing severe oppression by the Midianites. Food was scarce. Morale was low. Gideon and all the people of Israel were afraid and discouraged.

God appeared to Gideon. He encountered a scared young man who was threshing wheat in a winepress and said to him, "The LORD is with you, O mighty man of valor" (Judges 6:12). Gideon experienced God's presence and received an identity change. Gideon saw himself as insignificant and afraid. God saw Gideon as a man of courage and bravery. God promises to be with Gideon and move powerfully through him to rescue the oppressed Israelites.

Do you see the commissioning pattern? Gideon is chosen by God to encounter Him. In the presence of God, Gideon receives a new identity. Gideon was afraid and timid before encountering God. Now he is a brave and mighty warrior because God is with him. Gideon follows God. God blesses the Israelite people and rescues them from their oppressors, through Gideon.

God's presence and voice changed Gideon into a brave warrior who rescued his people from oppression.

ISAIAH: GO AND SAY TO THESE PEOPLE

Isaiah 6 records the prophet's commissioning encounter with God. It was a time of political instability because the king, Uzziah, had died. In this encounter with Jesus (check out John 12:41), Isaiah saw the King high and lifted up, reigning on a throne. Heavenly beings are worshiping God, crying out: "Holy, holy, holy is the LORD of hosts; the whole earth is full of His glory!" (Isaiah 6:3).

At this revelation, Isaiah immediately acknowledged his own sin and unworthiness. He confessed that he is sinful with impure speech and that the people of God are also full of impurity. One of the heavenly beings touched Isaiah's lips with a burning coal from the altar. Isaiah received a new identity as a righteous and pure spokesman for God. His guilt and sin were taken away and satisfied by God Himself.

Then Isaiah heard God ask His divine council, "Whom shall I send, and who will go for us?" Isaiah's immediate response was "Here I am! Send me" (Isaiah 6:8). He was commissioned in the presence of God to go and speak to the people.

Again, we see the commissioning pattern. Isaiah is chosen by God to encounter Him. In the presence of God, he receives a new identity. Isaiah was impure and guilty of sin before encountering God. Now his guilt is taken away and God is with him. Isaiah follows God and speaks the very words of Jesus to the people.

God's presence and voice changed Isaiah into a pure spokesman who faithfully declared the words of God to His people.

THE DISCIPLES: YOU WILL BE MY WITNESSES

After His resurrection, Jesus appeared to His disciples. Discouraged and afraid, the disciples believed that those who had killed Jesus were coming for them next. Knowing they were afraid, He said, "Peace be with you. As the Father has sent me, even so I am sending you." And then Jesus "breathed on them and said to them, 'Receive the Holy Spirit'" (John 20:21–22).

In Acts 1, right before His ascension back to heaven, Jesus said to these same disciples, "You will receive power when the Holy Spirit has come upon you, and you will be my witnesses in Jerusalem and in all Judea and Samaria, and to the end of the earth" (Acts 1:8). These men and women were afraid, but after encountering Jesus they became bold witnesses of His kingdom and good news.

The change was undeniable. Even the Jewish religious leaders noticed the change. Later in the book of Acts, Peter and John were questioned before the high priest in Jerusalem about healing a lame beggar in Jesus' name. The Bible records that when the Jewish religious leaders and scholars "saw the boldness of Peter and John, and perceived that they were uneducated, common men, they were astonished. And they recognized that they had been with Jesus" (Acts 4:13).

The disciples were commissioned in an encounter with the resurrected Jesus. This commissioning extends to all disciples of Christ, whom He commands to "Go therefore and make disciples of all nations, baptizing them in the name of the Father and of the Son and of the Holy Spirit, teaching them to observe all that I have commanded you. And behold, I am with you always, to the end of the age" (Matthew 28:19–20).

Again, we see the pattern of commissioning. Common, uneducated men and women encounter the risen Jesus. They are afraid, timid, and untrained compared to the religious scholars of Jerusalem. In the presence of Jesus, they receive His Holy Spirit and are empowered to speak and act with boldness in declaring the good news. They follow Jesus' leadership by the Holy Spirit and change the world.

God's presence and voice changed the disciples into bold and powerful witnesses of Jesus.

GOD'S WORKMANSHIP

The Father wants to do the same thing through you. Yes, you.

You may feel unfruitful, like Abraham, but Jesus wants to use you to bless generations of people.

You may feel afraid and timid, like Gideon, but Jesus wants to give you courage and His presence to accomplish His will through you.

You may feel unclean and unworthy and that you've gone too far with your sin, like Isaiah, but Jesus is standing ready to forgive and restore you to holiness. He will make you a mouthpiece for His good news.

Like the uneducated disciples, you may feel that you don't know enough about God or the Bible to be used by Jesus in a supernatural way, but Jesus wants to empower you by His Spirit to bring healing and restoration to those around you.

You may say, "Jamie, that's over the top. God used Abraham, Gideon, Isaiah, and the disciples in amazing ways, but He wouldn't do that through me. I didn't go to seminary. I've sinned a lot in my life. I'm too afraid of what people will think. I'm not what Jesus is looking for when He needs a leader."

Really? Are you sure about that? I believe those thoughts are limiting beliefs and they are not from Jesus.

Here's the truth about you. The Bible says, "For by grace you have been saved through faith. And this is not your own doing; it is the gift of God, not a result of works, so that no one may boast. For we are his workmanship, created in Christ Jesus for good works, which God prepared beforehand, that we should walk in them" (Ephesians 2:8–10).

Here's what that means for you. You are correct about your sin—you are not good enough for God to use in a significant way. But the good news is that the Father has chosen to make you righteous and pure by faith in Jesus! This isn't something you can pull off in your own strength; rather, it's a free gift given to you.

But that's not all. Also, before God created anything, He had you in mind and planned things for you to do and accomplish by His power. Before He spoke a single galaxy into being, the Father had specific assignments for you to walk in today.

This verse still astonishes me. I am stunned by the graciousness of the Father. Before creating time or matter or space, He knew we would sin against Him. He knew He would come in flesh to die for us. He knew the pain and agony of crucifixion. He knew the amazing things He wanted to accomplish through each and every one of us—including you.

This truth motivates me. I do not want to miss out on a single adventure that the Father planned for me since before the beginning of time itself! I want to experience Him in His fullness every day. I want to hear His voice and follow Him every day. I want to see the people He has planned to heal and redeem and set free by His Spirit through me! I don't want to miss a moment that the Father has planned for me since before the beginning of time.

Today is an adventure with Jesus. He has encounters planned for you this week. If you learn to walk with Him, be present, and follow His voice, you will see the miraculous. The Father planned these moments of adventure before He spoke the first atom into being. He planned to partner with you, today, to accomplish amazing things.

Will you join Him?

DO NOT MISS OUT

What your family needs most is for you to grow in friendship with God. They need you to practice the presence of the Father, receive His identity over your life, and walk with Him every day, sharing the kingdom as you go.

What your friends need is for you to prioritize God's presence in your life and walk with Him each day in His power. The Father has eternal fruit He has planned to produce in your life and then others through you.

Don't miss this. Don't miss out on assignments and supernatural moments appointed for you to accomplish with Jesus.

If you are a father or a mother, understand that the most important thing you can do for your kids is to regularly encounter Jesus, walk with Him daily, and show them what He is like in your life. Let them see, through you, how good the Father is.

Oftentimes, we will not see the effects in this life. We must trust that the Father has an eternal plan. You may never know the influence of your life on the generations after you, all because you chose to say to Jesus, "Here I am! Send me."

THE LASTING IMAGE OF MY PAWPAW

My paternal grandfather was nicknamed Pawpaw. He saw Jess and me get married but never met Bailey and Caden, his great-grandkids. He died before they were born. I wish they could've met my pawpaw. When I think of him, one singular image has burned its way into my memories.

Pawpaw would often come visit our family in Fort Worth, especially during holidays. Every day he stayed with us, around late morning my pawpaw would sit down at our kitchen table. He would open his leatherbound Bible, remove his hearing aids, read the Word, and encounter his Savior and Friend, Jesus.

This left an indelible mark on my young mind and heart. I realized that he took the hearing aids out to deafen the noise of my siblings and me running around the house shooting our Nerf bows and arrows at each other. But his consistent example of practicing the presence of God in the Word marked me. It became an example and model for me: this is how a godly man remains present with Jesus.

Every morning, if the weather is cooperating, I go to my screened-in back porch and commune with my Father. I sip coffee. I read the Word. I talk to my Father. I listen to Jesus speak truth over my life. I prepare to walk with the Holy Spirit the rest of the day. We talk together about my daily goals and schedule.

If the weather is bad, the encounter happens inside the house. This is a standing meeting between the Creator of the universe and me. This meeting is the most important thing on my schedule. This encounter with my God shapes the rest of my day. Every morning, when Bailey and Caden wake up and come downstairs, they see their dad on the porch, practicing the presence of his Friend and Savior, Jesus.

My pawpaw never knew what his example of practicing the presence of Jesus would do in my life or my kids' lives. When I see my pawpaw again, standing with Jesus, we will have a conversation about his life and the generational fruit that was borne from his simple pattern of being present with Jesus every day in front of his grandson. And if Jesus is okay with it, I may bring my Nerf bow and arrow too.

NORTH AMERICAN CHURCH CULTURE

One goal of this chapter is to motivate you to show up and be present with God and with others in your life. I want you to experience all the amazing assignments and plans that the Father desires to accomplish through you.

I've served in vocational church ministry for over twenty years and have noticed something about North American church culture. We as leaders, pastors, and teachers have allowed a Moses-model of ministry to dominate our churches.

Immediately following the giving of the Ten Commandments, we see an interesting moment between the people of God and Moses. The people see the presence of God on the mountain, and they are afraid. They tell Moses to go up on the mountain and talk to God for them because they are terrified to hear His voice for themselves (Exodus 20:18–21). They want Moses, their leader, to be a mediator of God's presence and voice for them.

That was the old covenant model of experiencing God and hearing His voice. During that time, you had to find a prophet or some other mediator to hear from God for you and tell you what God was saying. That is not how it is supposed to work today in the new covenant.

Through the prophet Jeremiah, God explains His plans for the new covenant. He says,

> This is the covenant that I will make with the house of Israel after those days, declares the LORD: I will put my law within them, and I will write it on their hearts. And I will be their God, and they shall be my people. And no longer shall each one teach his neighbor and each his brother, saying, "Know the LORD," for they shall all know me, from the least of them to the greatest, declares the LORD. For I will forgive their iniquity, and I will remember their sin no more. (Jeremiah 31:33–34)

In the new covenant, God intends to personally engage with each of us. After the resurrection of Jesus and the pouring out of the Holy Spirit upon His people, we no longer need a human mediator—Jesus is our mediator. God has put His Spirit inside us. Because of this, you and I can experience His presence and hear His voice today.

Friend, don't settle for a Moses-model Christianity. Don't wait for the pastor to go into the presence of God during the week and then come out on Sundays to declare to you what God is saying. No, you don't have to wait. Go get Him yourself! Get into His Word. Get into His presence. Talk to Jesus daily. Then lead others. Seminary training doesn't get you closer to God's heart or voice.

Remember the disciples? They were common, uneducated men and women whose only credentials were that they had been *with* Jesus. They shocked the religious scholars who, though they knew the Bible, couldn't see Jesus when He was in their presence.

Now, don't get me wrong here. I believe in preaching and teaching. I don't think we should abandon this communication medium; however, if church leaders teach in a way that implies they are the only ones who can really hear from God or understand Him, they are failing their call. (As a pastor, that includes me!)

The goal of kingdom leadership is to equip and encourage everyone around us to experience the Father, get in the Word, hear the voice of Jesus, and share with others what the Holy Spirit is revealing to them. This is the adventure of being on mission with the triune God.

Here are some practical steps you can take today to join this daily adventure with the triune God.

PRACTICAL STEPS

1. Show up every day with a "send me" posture. There is nothing passive about the kingdom of God. Show up. Wake up in the morning, and say to Jesus, "Here I am! Send me."

   What if Moses had never said "Here I am" to God at the burning bush? Well, God would have found another leader to accomplish His purposes. Don't miss what God wants to do through you. Someone you encounter today needs to hear and experience Jesus through you. The Father is looking for someone to go and represent Him today. Take a "send me" posture, and go. Don't wait for your pastor or someone more "qualified"—*you* go, today.

2. Receive revelation of your identity in the presence of Jesus. You may be afraid and timid. I have good news—so were Gideon, Joshua, Elijah, Timothy, and many more. What you feel about yourself and how you see yourself is not as important as what the Father sees.

    Ask Him what He thinks about you. Ask Him to give you an understanding of the identity He wants you to embrace and live out. Ask Him what plans He has for your day today. This is the priority meeting of your day: being with your Father, Jesus, and the Holy Spirit.

    All other meetings will be less effective if you miss this time of encountering and experiencing Him. This is a commissioning time, in His presence. You are joining in a long line of men and women who have prioritized being with Jesus and living their lives from His presence.

3. Finally, tell others what you have experienced or heard from Jesus. Look for opportunities during the day to share with someone what Jesus has revealed to you. Maybe you read something in the Bible that jumped off the page at you. Share that with someone during the day.

When I began to order my days this way, I was amazed at how many times someone would respond, "That's exactly what I needed to hear today!" or "How did you know I needed to hear this? Have you been stalking me on Facebook?"

Let this become a daily adventure between you and the triune God. Get in His presence and ask for revelation. Write down what you are hearing or seeing or learning. Then look for ways to share that revelation with family, friends, coworkers, or even strangers you meet.

By the way, I have created a companion *40-Day Journal* resource to help you put these steps into practice. You can find this companion journal online.

In the next chapter, we will explore what this looks like in both the life of Jesus and in some modern-day examples. We will examine the miraculous power of God working through someone who chooses to say, "Here I am! Send me."

Chapter Eleven

LIVING "DOUBLY" PRESENT

I am the vine; you are the branches. Whoever abides in me
and I in him, he it is that bears much fruit, for apart from
me you can do nothing.

– John 15:5

Have you ever wondered what Jesus would do at a sushi restaurant in Cincinnati?

In late August of 2019, I met some friends for lunch at a restaurant called Aroma in Cincinnati. The sushi was great, and our waitress was very kind. The Holy Spirit had been teaching me the principles in this chapter about being present with Jesus and the people around me. I was learning to be mindful of His presence and listen to what Jesus might be saying to me while I'm with others.

Midway through our meal, I looked at our waitress, who was refilling my water, and the Father brought to mind a family friend who is a schoolteacher; she adores kids, loves school, and is an excellent educator. This family friend has spent years accumulating many degrees in education. Additionally, she has suffered from chronic back pain. The Father also reminded me that a couple Christmases ago we prayed for her back and all her pain left.

With this in mind, I thought that the Father may want to say something through me to our waitress. At the end of the meal, I asked her if I could share something that I felt God wanted to say to her. She

115

smiled nervously and agreed. I shared that God is proud of her love for children and that this is a gift He has given her. He has created her uniquely to teach kids. As I shared this information, tears began to flow down her face. She smiled and thanked us for encouraging her. She was studying to be a teacher and had a really bad day at school that morning. She was amazed and touched by the Father's love and care for her!

"Do you happen to have back pain?" I then asked. She nodded and admitted she'd had chronic back pain. I asked if we could pray for her back, and she agreed. I asked her to put her hand on her back, right where it hurt. After asking permission to put my hand on her shoulder, I prayed a brief prayer of blessing and then commanded the pain to leave her body.

She said that she felt *nothing* after we prayed. All the pain was gone. She confessed that she'd been regularly in pain all day, from the moment she got out of bed in the morning. Working as a waitress only made it worse. She was *always* in pain. And now the pain was gone. Instantly. Smiling, I said, "Jesus loves you and has healed you! Isn't that awesome?"

I like sushi. But I love seeing Jesus minister to those around me. Especially at a sushi place in Cincinnati, Ohio.

JESUS' MINISTRY RHYTHM

Jesus' life and ministry are an instructive model for us as we seek to practice the presence of God out in the world. Jesus prioritized solitude with His Father in prayer, and then He would go from this solitude out into a hurting world. Jesus was present, alone, with the Father. Then He would go out into the world, carrying the presence of His Father with Him. Presence in solitude. Presence in public.

In the Gospel of Luke, we read that Jesus went up on a mountain and prayed all night to the Father. After this prayer time, He called His disciples and took them to minister with Him to a great crowd of people (Luke 6:12–19). The public ministry of Jesus flowed *from* His personal practice of the presence of the Father. And if the Creator of the universe needed that kind of rhythm, do you think we might need it too? Our public ministry to others will only be as effective as our personal practice of God's presence.

Let me be clear, though. This Jesus-rhythm is not the following pattern:

1. Get alone and pray.
2. Go out and minister until you are exhausted.
3. Retreat and rest in prayer again.
4. Rinse and repeat.

No, that's not actually what Jesus models for us. Jesus' practice of the presence of His Father wasn't separate from His ministry; rather, His ministry was to carry the Father's presence with Him out into the world.

The relationship between the Father and the Son grew (Luke 2:52) in personal prayer and continued in public ministry. Jesus explains this dynamic relational ministry-rhythm in the Gospel of John. After healing a paralyzed man at the pool of Bethesda on the Sabbath, Jesus was questioned by the religious leaders of His day. His response is instructive. Jesus said that He does nothing on His own but only what He sees the Father doing. Whatever He sees the Father doing, that's what He will do (John 5:1–19).

Jesus' ministry actions were driven by what He saw the Father doing around Him. Many people were sick at that pool, but only one paralyzed man was healed. How did Jesus know who to minister to? The Father showed Him.

Jesus was so connected to His Father, in both solitude and in public ministry, that He could see what the Father's plan was in the moment. Jesus did what He saw the Father doing. He walked in friendship with His Father, and supernatural ministry was the by-product.

Later, after being questioned again, Jesus responded, "I have not spoken on my own authority, but the Father who sent me has himself given me a commandment—what to say and what to speak" (John 12:49). Here we see that Jesus' very words are being directed by the Father, in the moment. He is speaking what He hears the Father saying. After the resurrection, Peter was explaining to a group of gentiles how Jesus ministered in such miraculous ways. He preached, "God anointed Jesus of Nazareth with the Holy Spirit and with power. He went about doing good and healing all who were oppressed by the devil, for *God was with him*" (Acts 10:38, emphasis mine).

The Father was *with* Jesus. He wasn't only with Him on the mountain in prayer but all the time. Jesus was present with the Father in public, listening and watching. His words and actions were directed by the Father.

Jesus was "doubly" present—fully present with the Father and fully present with the people around Him.

Being doubly present meant Jesus was listening "two-ways." For example, He listened to the Samaritan woman at the well, while He simultaneously listened to the Father for her. He heard the pain she carried from a string of broken relationships with men, though she never said those things out loud.

How did Jesus know? The Father told Him about her pain and showed Him to speak about living water. The rest is history. She becomes an evangelist for her town and tells everyone, "He told me everything about me!" (John 4:39, my paraphrase). Later, many from that gentile town came to believe in Jesus as the Savior of the world.

How did revival break out in this gentile town? Because Jesus was *doubly present.*

This is the ministry-rhythm of Jesus. Present with the Father. Present with others.

ABIDE IN ME

This ministry continues through His disciples then and now. We can live doubly present, just like Jesus. The priority in ministry is to stay connected relationally to the Father, Son, and Holy Spirit. From this relational communion with the triune God ministry flows to others.

Jesus taught this concept in John 15 using the metaphor of the vine and the branches. He said to the disciples, "Abide in me, and I in you. As the branch cannot bear fruit by itself, unless it abides in the vine, neither can you, unless you abide in me. I am the vine; you are the branches. Whoever abides in me and I in him, he it is that bears much fruit, for apart from me you can do nothing" (John 15:4–5). Jesus is the Vine. We are the branches. To bear fruit in the kingdom of God, we must abide in Him.

The verb *abide* means to stay or remain in the same place, to continue a certain condition or activity. We bear kingdom fruit when we continue to remain relationally connected to Jesus.

This sounds a lot like living in His presence all day, doesn't it? This sounds like what we've been talking about all throughout this book. We are created to abide in the Father, Son, and Holy Spirit. And our abiding directly affects the people around us. When we abide in Christ, the people around us experience the presence of Jesus through us.

What does that look like practically? Jesus explains in Luke 10 and gives a picture of abiding and fruit-bearing in the kingdom. He sent out his disciples in pairs, two by two. These pairs were to go from home to home looking for "people of peace." If they found people who were open to them, then they were to engage those specific people and their households. Jesus commanded His disciples to eat with these people, heal the sick in the house, and tell them, "The kingdom of God has come near to you" (Luke 10:8–9).

How could these disciples heal the sick? And how could these disciples say such a startling thing? They told the people that the kingdom of God had come near to them. How had the kingdom of God come near? The disciples were carrying the kingdom with them and were ambassadors of the King, Jesus. The kingdom of God had come near because the disciples carried the presence of the King with them.

The same is true for you and me. We get to carry His kingdom wherever we go because we have the King dwelling within us by the Holy Spirit! Wherever you go, you represent the King as His presence goes with you.

This means that the gas station can be a place for a God encounter. The kingdom of God can come near the person across from you at the gas pump because you are there, carrying the King's presence. The produce aisle of the grocery store can be the location of a kingdom encounter because you carry the King with you. You bring His kingdom and presence with you, everywhere you go, by being present with Jesus and those around you.

The goal is for others to experience the Father through us. They can come into a real relationship with Him by faith in Jesus and by the power of the Holy Spirit. Do not dismiss the value of carrying His presence into every situation.

KINGDOM ENCOUNTERS

In 2017, the church I was serving began to take seriously the call of Jesus to find people of peace in our neighborhood. We figured that if Jesus commanded His disciples to go out and share the gospel, then we should probably do that too.

During that year, we had amazing encounters where Jesus healed many people. They were healed in their backs, shoulders, knees, feet, wrists, and many other areas. We even witnessed a cancerous tumor healed after praying for a woman in a city park next to the playground. Jesus healed her of cancer while her grandkids laughed and played on the monkey bars. We prayed for another woman who was blinded in one eye from a surgical accident where her optic nerve was severed by doctors. She felt a "pop," and her eyesight returned. After regaining her eyesight, she smiled and said, "Thank You, Jesus, for healing my blindness!"

Some of these encounters led to conversions as individuals experienced the Father's love and came to faith in Jesus as their Savior and Lord. In December of 2017, we visited the apartments behind our church building to find people of peace and pray for them. In one unit, we met a young father and began to talk with him. During the conversation, I was listening to the Holy Spirit and asking Him questions about the young dad.

The Spirit is a great teacher and guide, and He told me some important things about this young man. Standing on the balcony of this second-floor apartment, I shared with the young father what I believed the heavenly Father was telling me about him. He was touched and surprised by this. We prayed for his family, specifically his daughter, and then we left.

In January of 2018, I found a note under our church door from this young father, telling us how encouraged he was by our visit and that he wanted to sit and chat with me about some things. We met in my office at church, and the young man gave his life to Jesus. He repented of his sin and received new life by faith in Jesus' death and resurrection.

Before too long, he got a job in another city and moved out of our neighborhood. This young father had an encounter with the living

God because a couple of people decided to take Jesus' words seriously and go out, carrying the presence of the King with them. We could truthfully say, "The kingdom of God has come near you," because the King was with us.

Here are some practical steps you can take to abide in Jesus and bear kingdom fruit, today.

PRACTICAL STEPS

1. Be relationally present with the people around you. It is important to be mindful of whether you are emotionally and spiritually present with the people around you. It's possible to be physically present but not relationally present. Honestly, this is a challenge for me. I am easily distracted. I confess that I am easily bored by some people. Shamefully, I find myself wishing they would stop talking so I could go do something else.

   Am I the only one? I have a suspicion that this is true of some of you too. Disconnection is all around us. How many times have you been eating at a restaurant, watching a group of people all together physically but each on their individual phones? They are all physically present but not relationally present. How about you?

   Here's what I've learned. Put the phone down. Look at the people around you. Look into their eyes and engage at an emotional level. Ask the Father to give you His heart of compassion for them.

   Remember, the Father loves them and created them in His image. They are worthy of our attention. If we will just put the phone down, stop, and be present, we might just see the supernatural power of God break out around us. The Father loves them. Ask Him to give you His heart of love for them too.

2. Be "doubly" present with Jesus while you are present with others. Practice the presence of God even while in a conversation with family, coworkers, friends, and other strangers you meet.

I am a visual person, and this can be challenging for me. It is much easier to focus on the one thing I can see rather than on the Spirit of Jesus, which I cannot see with my natural eyes.

Here are some helpful tips. Picture Jesus standing or sitting next to the person or next to yourself. Again, our imagination is a gift from God, so use it. Ask Jesus questions, and start listening "two-ways." It will take some time to develop this skill, but you can start to practice double listening. While you are listening to the person in front of you, begin to ask Jesus, "What do You think about this situation? How do You see this person? What is their unique identity, and what gifts have You given them?"

Don't be surprised with what Jesus will tell you about the person or the situation in front of you. This is a wonderful benefit of being a friend of Jesus. Because we are His friends, He will make known to us what the Father is saying.

Jesus said to His disciples, "No longer do I call you servants, for the servant does not know what his master is doing; but I have called you friends, for all that I have heard from my Father I have made known to you" (John 15:15). Friends of Jesus get to hear the heart of the Father for others, just like Jesus did.

3.   Pray silently while talking with people, and ask the Holy Spirit to manifest His presence around you. Most of the people you encounter day-to-day are stressed, anxious, and feel unloved.

While staying relationally present, pray and ask the Holy Spirit to bring peace over the person. I've lost count of the number of times that people report experiencing peace when they talk with me or hear me speak. Is this because I'm some peace magician or have some gift? No. It's because I carry the Prince of Peace with me and I regularly pray that He manifest peace to the people around me. With my eyes open, I silently pray for those I am with. I pray that they would experience peace and the presence of the Father, through me. I ask the Holy Spirit to manifest His presence upon them while we talk together.

You can also pray for wisdom. Remember, Jesus only said what He heard the Father saying in a particular moment. We need wisdom to not just blurt out whatever we think we might be hearing. For example, what if the Holy Spirit showed you a secret pain in the heart of the person in front of you? Or some secret sin in their life? Should you blurt out what you are seeing or hearing? No, that's not wisdom. We need a little emotional intelligence and the wisdom of Jesus to know what to say and when to say it.

Ask the Spirit for wisdom to know how to speak or if you need to be quiet and pray for this pain. This has happened many times to me. Jesus will show me someone's pain, and this prompts me to pray for them. Sometimes, I never tell them what I've heard. I simply pray for them. Just because the Holy Spirit points something out doesn't give me a green light to start saying things to people. Pray for wisdom.

4. Finally, speak or serve in the power of the Spirit. Spiritual gifts are an important topic, and I want to tackle them in a later book. I've chosen not to address them fully here; however, there is one helpful framework to consider.

   The Bible contains multiple lists of spiritual gifts. There is a list of gifts in Romans 12 and two lists in 1 Corinthians 12. Many people get caught up on these lists and want to know what their "gift" is and how to use it.

   That's a good desire, and we should encourage that. However, Peter gives a simple framework and way to think about spiritual gifts. He divides all gifts into two categories: *speaking* and *serving*. Here's how he explains it: "As each has received a gift, use it to serve one another, as good stewards of God's varied grace: whoever speaks, as one who speaks oracles of God; whoever serves, as one who serves by the strength that God supplies—in order that in everything God may be glorified through Jesus Christ. To him belong glory and dominion forever and ever. Amen" (1 Peter 4:10–11).

   Here we see that spiritual gifts are a way we can love each other in the areas of either speaking or serving. So, let's apply this to living doubly present. If Jesus begins to speak to you about the person in front of you, begin to either speak to them or serve them, in love.

When we speak, we are to speak "as one speaking the very words of God" (1 Peter 4:11 NRSV). That sounds like Jesus, doesn't it? Remember how He explained it: "I only say what I hear the Father saying." When we serve, we are to serve "by the strength that God supplies." That sounds like Jesus too. He only did what He saw the Father doing.

When you regularly practice this kind of speaking and serving, you will see the supernatural power of God flow through you. I promise.

Go for it. Be doubly present, and watch what God will do through you!

One final thing for us to consider. The presence of God isn't just about you and God alone. You were created to be with others too. In our last chapter, we will explore what it means to be a community of presence.

Chapter Twelve

COMMUNITY
OF PRESENCE

For where two or three are gathered in my name,
there am I among them.

— Matthew 18:20

Fall is my favorite season. There is football, crisp weather, autumn colors, family, and the climax of Thanksgiving. Food. Family. Togetherness. There is something "right" about being together with people we love, preparing a great meal, and eating together. It's almost like we were created for this!

When my family gathers for Thanksgiving, everyone brings something for the meal and works together to prepare the feast. One couple is peeling potatoes. Another is working on frying the turkey. Older cousins are playing with and entertaining the younger ones. The Dallas Cowboys are playing on TV. Preparations are underway for a great feast and time together as family.

The pinnacle is the meal itself. Dish after dish fills the table, even crowding out the plates. We fill up for the first round of food and begin to eat. We tell stories. We laugh. Many times, it's been a while since we've all been together, so the time is invaluable. We catch up on the things that have happened since our last meal together. We drink. We eat. We smile.

But family gatherings are never perfect. Even in my family. In some families, the meal is not full of food and laughter and working together.

Sometimes unspoken hurts, bitterness, and passive aggressiveness are present. Rather than working together to prepare the meal, some members of the family are watching the game or on their phones while one or two of the moms do all the food prep. Unfortunately, those same moms will do all the clean-up afterward too.

Something inside us knows this isn't right. You know what I mean?

We know that our family gatherings should be joyful and peaceful, but at times they are stressful and anxious. We know we should laugh and be honest with one another, but instead we put on fig leaves. We hide our true selves and then feel unknown by our family. Or we speak our "truth," which is really meant to lash out and injure the hearer.

Our conversations should be joyful and life-giving but instead are either passive-aggressive or just aggressive-aggressive. Parents are hurt and distant from their kids. Siblings are upset and frustrated with each other.

Some members of the family try to dominate the conversation, especially involving politics. Other members are quiet and thinking, "How long do I have to stay here? Why does she keep talking? I can't wait to get away from these people!"

For some, the holidays are difficult because they are alone. A table that should be full of food and laughter is barren and silent. For others, the recent death of a loved one causes more pain during these meals.

Regret. Loneliness. Pain. Something inside of us knows this isn't right! Something is wrong. We are disconnected. We are hurt. We are not our true selves with each other. We ignore each other. We blame each other. We feel shame and are desperate to cover those feelings with anything to make us feel better. We gather together but are covered in fig leaves. We are present but hiding.

WHY DO WE FEEL THIS TENSION?

We feel this tension deep down because we were created for joyful intimacy with others. We were created to be fully ourselves—the best of ourselves—with everyone we meet. We were created for friendship with God and others without fig leaves. No pretending. No posturing. No anxiety. No abuse. No disconnection.

You were created for friendship and a perfect community, where you are known and loved. You were created to be in a perfect community because you were created *by* a perfect community. That perfect community is the Trinity: Father, Son, and Holy Spirit.

No jealousy exists between the three persons of the Trinity. There is no disconnection, nor are there fig leaves. There is only joyful togetherness. You and I were created for this same joyful freedom and togetherness with God and others.

When we don't experience freedom, we are reminded of the fall. Adam was afraid of God, so he hid. Adam and Eve experienced shame in each other's presence because of their sin and covered themselves with fig leaves. Adam blamed God *and* Eve for his sin. He refused to take responsibility for his actions, so Adam blamed his wife and the God who gave her to him. Can you imagine how that next conversation at breakfast went between the first couple? Do you think there was frustration, hurt, anger, bitterness, and a feeling of rejection? Yep.

They felt just the same way you and I do when we experience being stabbed in the back and hurt by those around us, which only breeds distrust of others. We distance ourselves to protect ourselves. We put on fig leaves and masks to cover our feelings of shame. We may be physically present but not *truly* present with others.

So, what do we do about this? *Can* we do anything about this? Let's look at God and see what He thinks about this problem.

THE IMPORTANCE OF THE TABLE

God loves food. God loves friendship. God loves eating around a table with new and old friends. God loves telling stories and laughter. God loves the unity and peace found at a table with a great meal. God loves a family party.

How do I know this? Because Jesus is the exact representation of the Father (Hebrews 1:3). That means that Jesus' actions and behaviors show us how God acts and behaves. Seeing Jesus is seeing the Father because they are one (John 14:9–10). Whatever Jesus is doing is what the Father is doing too.

Have you noticed one of the main things Jesus did while He was here? Remember, He only had three years of ministry to save the world from sin and declare the good news of the kingdom. So, what was Jesus doing?

He was eating at a table with friends. He was talking, around a table, with sinners and tax collectors. He was teaching—at meals. He was healing—in homes before and after meals. He was inviting Himself over to eat at the homes of sinners and tax collectors. Jesus' assignment was to rescue the world from sin and death, and His primary mode of ministry was eating and talking to friends around a table.

Do you remember Jesus' first miracle? What was the first "sign" that Jesus performed to communicate to the entire world what God is like? We read in John 2:1–11 that Jesus was at a wedding. The party ran out of wine. Shame and dishonor would be attached to this groom and family for the rest of their lives if word got out that the wine was gone.

So the Creator of galaxies chose to turn water into wine as His first miracle. His first sign that communicated to people that "God is here among you" was at a feast. His mom kind of pushed Him into it, but Jesus still chose to rescue a wedding from shame and dishonor. His first miracle was at a wedding party. A celebration of love and union.

And He didn't stop there. He kept hanging out with sinners at meals around tables. Jesus was so known for this table ministry that the religious leaders accused Him of being a drunk, a glutton, and a friend of sinners (Luke 7:34). Of course, Jesus never was drunk or gluttonous, but He was a friend of sinners.

You see, in Jesus' time, to eat with someone communicated friendship, approval, and intimacy. The religious leaders would have never been caught dead eating with a tax collector or a prostitute. Why? Because eating at the same table with sinners meant you approved of them and were identifying yourself with them. The religious would never eat with "those kinds of people." But Jesus came and identified with sinners by eating with them.

He talked with them and listened to their stories. He laughed and ate with them, aware of their pain and shame. He was present with them at the table. These men and women experienced the presence of God as He sat down and had a meal with them. These sinners encountered grace at the table with Jesus. They experienced friendship with God at a table.

THIS IS MY BODY, WHICH IS GIVEN FOR YOU

Another important event occurred around a table. On the night He was to be betrayed, Jesus sat with His disciples and ate a meal. He ate with friends, even sitting with the one who would betray Him (Matthew 26:25; John 13:26).

Jesus took bread, gave thanks for it, broke it, and gave it to His friends. He said, "This is my body, broken for you. Eat this and remember me." Then Jesus took a cup and said, "This is my blood of the new covenant, poured out for many, for the forgiveness of sins. Drink it in remembrance of me" (1 Corinthians 11:23–25, my paraphrase).

Jesus established a pattern of eating, drinking, and remembering grace at a table. He was present with them at the table, and he established this rhythm for all his followers. The early church was formed at Pentecost (Acts 2) when the Holy Spirit came and filled the disciples while they were all together in the same place. They were probably eating at a table together since Pentecost is one of the celebratory feasts of Israel that includes a meal.

After the Pentecost event, Luke records the regular practice of the early church like this:

> And they devoted themselves to the apostles' teaching and the fellowship, to the breaking of bread and the prayers. And awe came upon every soul, and many wonders and signs were being done through the apostles. And all who believed were together and had all things in common. And they were selling their possessions and belongings and distributing the proceeds to all, as any had need. And day by day, attending the temple together and breaking bread in their homes, they received their food with glad and generous hearts, praising God and having favor with all the people. And the Lord added to their number day by day those who were being saved. (Acts 2:42–47)

We see that the regular rhythm of this new community was to eat together and be together in the name of Jesus Christ. This rhythm of life together—present with Jesus—changed the world. And His presence with His people is still changing the world today.

The early church regularly studied the words of Jesus together and prayed together, in their homes, around a table. They would attend the temple services and then return to their homes to break bread and eat together with glad and generous hearts. The presence of Jesus, by the Holy Spirit, was so powerful among them that many were physically healed and set free of demon possession. Daily they were gathering around the table and adding to their number those who were saved by faith in Jesus. The table was growing as more and more sinners encountered Jesus in His people, at the table, eating together.

So What?

Why am I taking so much time here? Why devote the last chapter to this subject? Well, we encounter the presence of God uniquely with others. Much of this book could be read individually and separate from a community, but without community there are aspects of God's presence we cannot experience.

It is true, you can encounter God by yourself. It is not true, however, that you can encounter all of God by yourself. You need community with others to experience God in all His fullness (Ephesians 1:22–23; 3:14–19).

The presence of God is uniquely experienced with other friends of Jesus, together. That is one of the reasons the church is called the "body" of Christ. In community, with each other, Jesus is present. We are dependent on one another. And together we are uniquely Jesus to the world and each other.

Community is messy business because we are messy people. Fig leaves and sin keep us from drawing near to one another in unity and love. We hide from community with others, afraid of being exposed. We get into community and then hurt each other with sin and fig leaves.

Honestly, it is hard to be vulnerable with others. It is hard to risk being stabbed in the back by a "friend." Jesus knows the feeling. He gave three years to a community of friends. One of them betrayed Him. The rest abandoned Him. Only one was present at His crucifixion. Still, He calls us to risk vulnerability in community and to experience His presence together. Jesus calls us to receive grace and extend grace, at the table, with others. It is in the vulnerable exchange of grace and forgiveness that we encounter Jesus, together.

Where two or more friends of Jesus are gathered together, He is uniquely among us (Matthew 18:20). Here are some practical steps you can take today to experience the fullness of God's presence within a community.

PRACTICAL STEPS

1. Understand the value and potential of your family table. This table provides an opportunity to be present with your immediate family, friends, and others. Fast food is an amazing gift for busy parents and families, but it is a terrible thing for our souls and waists.

    I'm writing this book during the summer of 2020, and the coronavirus has forced families to slow down and eat together again at the table. This is a gift, even amid a challenging and painful season. My family has enjoyed the forced rhythm of eating together in the evenings. I pray that this is a rhythm we will not lose when life goes back to "normal."

    Parents, be present with your kids at the table. Put the phones down, look each other in the eye, and engage relationally. Jesus is there among you at your table. Invite Him to teach you how to be present as family, with Him.

    Read the Bible together, and ask the Holy Spirit for guidance. Discuss highs and lows from the day. Be present with each other and with Jesus. He is ready and willing to encounter your family at your table. Your home can be a place of encountering His presence. Do not neglect this powerful gift.

2. Invite others to join your table like the early church did. Is this scary? Yes. Will your house be messy and imperfect? Yes. Will Jesus show up even if you are scared and your house isn't immaculate? Yes. He loves to eat and be with you in community.

    This is the pattern of Jesus' church, His "body." Remember, they gathered in homes. They ate together. They studied Jesus' words together. They shared with each other. They listened to

God for each other and with each other. They became family—together. They went to the temple and then returned to their homes together. They invited "outsiders" to join them at the table. Those who had yet to encounter Jesus' grace met Him in His gathered people around the table.

Allow your table to grow as you invite others to join you. Invite them. Practice His presence with them. Listen to Jesus for them. Teach them how to listen to the Good Shepherd too. At your table they may experience Jesus so radically that they will worship Him and declare, "God is really here!" (1 Corinthians 14:24–25). Yes, the kingdom of God can come near to those who eat at your table too (Luke 10:9).

3. Finally, incorporate "the Lord's Table" into your regular rhythms as a community. Regularly celebrate the forgiveness of sins, through the body and blood of Jesus, at your table during a meal. This celebration of Communion is participation and fellowship with Jesus, together (1 Corinthians 10:16).

    Many at your table are discouraged and desperate for good news. At the table our sin, brokenness, shame, and pain meet the Savior of the world. It is a tangible and Spirit-filled symbol of forgiveness where we as prodigals are adopted back into the Father's family, by grace, through faith in the Son.

    For those struggling to forgive themselves for past or current sin patterns, the Lord's Table is a place of grace, forgiveness, and healing.

    For those struggling with isolation, loneliness, and abandonment, the Lord's Table is a place of fellowship and intimacy with both the triune God and a family of believers.

    For those struggling with obsessive cycles of thought patterns, the Lord's Table is a place to intentionally focus our minds on Christ in thanksgiving, remembrance, and proclamation of good news.

    For those struggling with hopelessness, the Lord's Table is a place of longing and anticipation for a future eternal hope.

Jesus promises to be present with you at the table. But there is one more thing about the table.

THE WEDDING TABLE TO COME

Jesus is coming back. When He returns, He will destroy all evil and even death itself. He will wipe away every tear from the eyes of His people. There will be no more sorrow, pain, crying, shame, fig leaves, sin, or even death (Revelation 21:3–4). He will come and dwell with us forever.

And that means there will be a party, a feast. There will be a celebration. There will be a table where we will sit and eat in friendship and unity. This will be a wedding table.

Jesus' first miracle was at a wedding feast, turning water into wine. He took away shame and replaced it with joy. When Jesus returns and conquers all evil at the end, He will celebrate with us at a wedding feast. He has taken our shame and sin and will replace it with the joy of His presence forever.

That is what's coming. That is what we look forward to when we gather and eat together. We remember and look forward to that day.

Jesus is waiting for that day too. On that same night when He established this meal of remembrance at the table, Jesus said, "I will not drink again of this [cup] until that day when I drink it new with you in My Father's kingdom" (Matthew 26:29).

Jesus is waiting in anticipation to sit and eat and drink with you in eternity. He waits, in excitement, to eat with you. He has a place waiting for you and me, forever. There is a place at the Father's table with your name on it purchased by Jesus Himself.

When that day comes, we will be eternally present with the Father, Jesus, and the Holy Spirit. We will see His face. We will hear His voice. We will walk with Him—together.

We will be friends with Him, forever. *Together.*

Conclusion

WALKING IN FRIENDSHIP WITH GOD

Enoch walked faithfully with God; then he was no more,
because God took him away.

– Genesis 5:24 (NIV)

By faith Enoch was taken from this life, so that he did not
experience death: "He could not be found, because God
had taken him away." For before he was taken, he was
commended as one who pleased God. And without faith it
is impossible to please God, because anyone who comes to
him must believe that he exists and that he rewards those
who earnestly seek him.

– Hebrews 11:5–6 (NIV)

You please God by walking with Him.

Enoch "pleased God" because he walked with God. The Greek translation (called the Septuagint) of the Hebrew text in Genesis 5:24 translates "walked with God" as "pleased God." Literally and grammatically, walking with God equals pleasing Him.

The Bible says that Enoch walked with God and then he was "no more" because God took him. Can you imagine that? You are walking with God, enjoying His presence, and talking with Him as a friend. Then you are taken to heaven to be in His presence.

What do you think happened next? Maybe Enoch opened his eyes in heaven and saw Jesus face-to-face. Then, perhaps, he gave his Savior a bear hug, and they continued their walk and conversation together—as friends.

When it is my time to see Jesus face-to-face, I want to go like Enoch. I want to be walking with Jesus and be in mid-conversation with Him at my last breath. Then I will open my eyes and see Him in person. We will embrace and then continue our conversation, forever, as friends.

How about you?

If you are still reading to this point, you are to be commended. Yet many of us read a book like this and then go away unchanged. Friend, don't do that this time.

This is a holy moment. As I mentioned earlier, this book may be a burning bush for you. Jesus is trying to get your attention, right now. He has been speaking to you throughout these burning words. Have you sensed His heat on these pages? He has been pursuing friendship with you.

Will you stop to see what this burning bush is all about? Will you change your daily routine to engage with the Father, Son, and Holy Spirit? I am praying that you will.

Here are two practical next steps to walking in friendship with God.

1. Commit to grow in friendship with God. Take the next forty days to establish a new rhythm of presence, conversation, and adventure with Jesus.

   Every day, show up to be with Him. When you get up in the morning, say to Jesus, "Here I am. Speak, Lord. Send me!" Put the practical steps from each chapter into practice for the next forty days. Develop new habits, and watch how your life is changed by the presence, voice, and power of God in your life.

   For forty days, schedule time to be with God. Get into the Bible and read it, relationally. Listen to Jesus speak over you and shape your identity. Share what you are hearing and learning from the Holy Spirit with one other person for forty days.

   I have created a companion resource called *The 40-Day Journal* to accompany this book. It is available online. The journal is designed to help you practice this new rhythm of walking in friendship with God. This resource provides forty Scriptures for you to reflect on with space to journal your reflections and what you are hearing from God as you listen. Each day, you will read a Scripture, be still, and listen to what Jesus may say to you.

2. Engage with your community on this adventure. Invite a friend or two to join you on this forty-day friendship with God journey. We all need accountability and encouragement to make any lasting change in our lives. If you are in a small group at church, invite them to join you for the next forty days.

    If you don't have a group, reach out to me directly. Seriously, I want to be an encouragement to you and help you grow in friendship with God. You can connect with me on Facebook, or YouTube or email me at jamie@jamiemoore.org.

    As a reminder, I have created a free chapter-by-chapter discussion guide and video course to go with this book. The discussion guide goes deeper, with application questions and a helpful recommended reading list. In the video course, I walk you through the concepts in the book and help you practically apply them in your daily life.

Friendship with God is available to you *today*.

The Father is pursuing you *today*.

Jesus loves you and wants to talk with you *today*.

The Holy Spirit wants to move through you *today*.

Walking in friendship pleases God. Walking in friendship with God will please you too.

Friend, I encourage you to take off the shame coverings and come out of hiding. Practice the relational presence of God, and receive His peace in every circumstance of your life. Talk to Jesus and allow His words to shape you with His identity over your life. Join the Holy Spirit on the adventure of what He has planned to accomplish through you today.

These are the three ingredients for you to become a friend of God: time, conversation, and activity—together with Him as your friend.

You will join a long line of God's friends who walked with Him and pleased Him. Walk in friendship with God today.

ACKNOWLEDGMENTS

Thank you to my wife, Jess. You are one of the Father's greatest gifts to me. Thanks for your loving support—and challenge when I've needed it. Thank you to my kiddos, Bailey and Caden. I am proud of the people you are becoming in Christ. I lubbers you.

Thank you to my parents, Stan and Mary Moore. You both taught me to trust God with all my heart and seek His glory above all else. I would not be where I am today without your love and example.

Thank you to the faith-families that have loved me so well! University Baptist, you laid the foundation for most of who I am today. Shiloh Baptist, you taught me to lead, even when I was afraid. Ridglea Baptist, you gave me the confidence I needed to enter full-time ministry. Trinity Baptist, you were the family we needed when we left "home." You will always be in our hearts. Sequoyah Hills, you taught me how to rely on the Father for everything. Mariemont, you have embraced us with open arms. You are family. Thank you.

Thank you to Chad Norris, Theresa Harris, and the Bridgeway Church Family for investing in me and Jess. Much of what I have said here in this book was taught to me by the Holy Spirit, through both of you.

Thank you to A. W. Tozer, even though we never met. I encountered your fire and burning heart exactly when I needed to. Thank you for your faithfulness to the Word and the Spirit of God. I want to love God more than anyone of my generation, because you did.

OTHER BOOKS BY JAMIE MOORE

Friendship with God: Discover God's Relational Presence and Receive Peace, Identity, and Purpose for Your Life

Friendship with God: Discussion Guide and 40-Day Journal

ABOUT THE AUTHOR

Jamie Moore is an elder and pastor at Mariemont Community Church in Cincinnati, Ohio. He holds degrees in music, worship, and theology from Baylor University, Southwestern Baptist Theological Seminary, and B. H. Carroll Theological Institute. His PhD dissertation was on the theology and ministry of A. W. Tozer. Jamie's passion is to help others grow in deep friendship with the Father, Son, and Holy Spirit.

For over twenty years, Jamie has served local churches in Texas, Tennessee, and Oklahoma, before coming to Ohio. Raised in Texas, Jamie is a huge fan of the Baylor Bears, Dallas Cowboys, Texas Rangers, and Dallas Mavericks. He and his wife, Jess, have two kids, Bailey and Caden, and trained together as a family to become black belts in tae kwon do.

If interested in having Jamie speak at one of your upcoming events, you can submit a speaking request at www.jamiemoore.org.

THE POWER OF YOUR REVIEW

Thank You for Reading My Book!

If *Friendship with God* spoke to you and was a source of encouragement, then would you please consider writing a review of my book?

This is encouraging to me and will help potential readers find out about the book as well!

Thank you for reading and reviewing.

May the Father bless you with His presence, His peace in Jesus, and His power through the Holy Spirit. May you enjoy deep friendship with the triune God, both now and throughout eternity.

Much love to you,

Jamie

NOTES

1   C. S. Lewis, *The Weight of Glory: And Other Addresses* (New York: HarperOne, 2001), 26.

2   A. W. Tozer, *That Incredible Christian: How Heaven's Children Live on Earth* (Camp Hill, PA: WingSpread, 1964), 72.

3   Jackie Salo, "6-year-old boy risks his life to save sister from brutal dog attack," *NY Post*, July 15, 2020, https://nypost.com/2020/07/15/6-year-old-boy-risks-life-to-save-sister-from-brutal-dog-attack.

4   Used by permission of Beckenhorst Press, Inc.

5   https://www.youtube.com/watch?v=hU_mBzCpUJ4